MASTERING

Betfair

PETE NORDSTED

HARRIMAN HOUSE LTD

3A Penns Road
Petersfield
Hampshire
GU32 2EW
GREAT BRITAIN

Tel: +44 (0)1730 233870
Fax: +44 (0)1730 233880
Email: enquiries@harriman-house.com
Website: www.harriman-house.com

First edition published in Great Britain in 2009 by Harriman House.

The right of Pete Nordsted to be identified as the author has been asserted
in accordance with the Copyright, Design and Patents Act 1988.

978-1-906659-02-8

British Library Cataloguing in Publication Data
A CIP catalogue record for this book can be obtained from the British Library.

Printed and bound in Great Britain by Marston Book Services Ltd, Oxfordshire

Designated trademarks and brands are the property of their respective owners.

Contents

Preface

What this book covers

This book explains my approach to trading on the Betfair markets and includes many of the strategies I regularly use in the sporting markets.

It covers the disciplined process that I go through before placing any trade. You will find highlighted throughout the book a set of trading rules (which are summarised at the end of the book).

Although this book does not cover horse racing it does cover many low-risk, high-return strategies for all the other major sporting markets available to trade on Betfair.

Who this book is for

This book is not intended to be an introductory guide to Betfair for beginners. The book does cover briefly some introductory concepts, but if you are new to Betfair then you should refer first to the excellent online help pages provided on Betfair's own website.

This book is written for the sports trader who is at the stage where he would like to take his trading to the next level.

It is also hoped that traders with a financial background may also, through reading this book, become aware of the many unique and profitable opportunities that trading the Betfair markets has to offer.

The book is written in plain English and I have attempted to get straight to the point of the matter while avoiding any confusing jargon. Throughout the book I relate my own personal experiences, either from my own trading or the training of my clients.

How the book is structured

The book has six main parts:

Part One – Getting Started

The first section of the book begins with what you need to know to put on a basic trade and highlights some of the disciplines you will need to acquire before you start trading seriously. There is also a section on the software and hardware requirements that need to be considered. This part of the book is very much aimed at the novice trader.

Part Two – The Trading Process

This section takes you through the process of deciding what trading systems and plans you are going to employ in your trading, and also discusses the advantages of back-testing. This section also deals with overtrading – a major error of inexperienced traders.

Part Three – Money Management and Risk

This covers the much neglected subject of money management and deals with subjects such as how much money a trader should be risking on an individual trade, and how to protect and preserve hard-earned capital.

Part Four – Trading Psychology

The fourth part of the book highlights various psychological issues such as learning to deal with losses, thinking outside the box and finding your own time frame as well as dealing with issues such as keeping yourself in the right physical shape to trade.

Part Five – Strategies

In the fifth part I share some of the strategies that I am currently using in the market. This includes sections on football, cricket, golf and tennis.

Part Six – The Rules for Mastering Betfair

As previously explained, throughout the book I highlight a series of essential rules to follow, these are summarised in this final part.

Charts

Throughout the book there are charts of betting prices. For more information on these charts please see the Appendix.

Introduction

How I got started with Betfair

I was first introduced to Betfair whilst serving in Afghanistan in 2003. One of my colleagues asked me if I had heard about the betting exchanges and what I thought of his system. I had heard of the term *betting exchange* through watching *At The Races* on Channel 4, but I didn't have a clue what they were or how they operated.

My friend explained to me that you can *lay* horses in a race. In other words you could bet against the horse winning – basically, he was looking to be the bookmaker.

I can remember logging on that first time in Kandahar and thinking that this did look interesting; but the internet connection was so poor we could not take it any further. However, it caught my imagination enough for me to explore the Betfair site upon returning home a week or so later. I was not new to gambling as in the early 1980s I had worked in a bookmakers taking and settling bets, but since leaving there had not been an active better. I had seen too many people gamble away their incomes and I believed there were more profitable places to put my hard-earned money.

On my return to the UK I immediately went about opening a Betfair account and started playing around by laying a few horses at minimum stakes. I believe after a few days of laying up to three horses a race I had roughly broken even. However, whilst playing around with the site I found I was becoming very interested in how the prices on the sporting markets moved whilst an event was still playing.

My first real trade came in a football match between Sunderland and Reading. I was just experimenting. Sunderland were 1-0 up in the game and I put £10 on them to win at something like 1.59 (I'll explain these prices later). As the game progressed and the minutes ticked by, I noticed that the Sunderland price was falling. It was at this moment my wife announced that she was ready to go out! Sunderland's price was now around 1.45. I didn't know what to do, but decided to lay them at 1.46. After doing this I realised that I was going to win £1.30 if Sunderland won, and lose nothing if it ended a draw or a Reading win. This got me very interested. Needless to say, that afternoon my mind was not on the shopping but on how I could get what I had found to work for me.

Green up

After doing some further research I then discovered that you can *green up*, which means you can show a profit no matter what the result. It was then that my trading increased and I would trade on anything at anytime. I would search the internet looking for radio coverage of sports such as Australian rules football. I was depositing £20 and by trading a few markets was hoping to turn it into £40. I really enjoyed my initiation on Betfair, and after further research into various sports I was becoming fairly successful, with both my staking and my confidence growing in tandem.

The shock of a large loss

Then all of a sudden I suffered a large loss in a Carling Cup tie between Crewe and Manchester United (the grisly details are explained later in the book). This had a big impact on my confidence and took the wind out of my sails. Previous to this setback I regarded Betfair as almost a licence to print money!

After suffering this loss I realised that up to then I had been lucky and in all truth was undisciplined in my trading. It was at this time that I decided to step back, take stock, and learn how to trade properly. I can remember reading on the Betfair forums 'Troy McClure', a successful Betfair trader, replying to a posting that posed the question,

"How do you win on Betfair?"

and Troy replied

"Just study and learn the markets for 12 months then act on what you find, that was the key to my success."

Just reading this posting on the Betfair forum altered my outlook completely, and I decided to change my approach.

A disciplined approach

It was about this time that I started reading *Trading in the Zone* and *The Disciplined Trader* by Mark Douglas. These books completely changed my attitude and approach to trading, both in the sporting and financial markets, and as a result I now trade successfully on probability and price alone.

These books by Mark Douglas are written for the financial markets. However, trading is trading and the general gist is pertinent: once you enter the market anything can happen and generally does, it is how well you handle this psychologically and emotionally that will ultimately determine your success. Once you've mastered this, it then suggests you use a mechanical trading plan and never divert from this plan.

It was also at this time that I decided to start studying market movements in depth. I soon came to the conclusion that simply backing short-priced favourites in sports such as darts, snooker and tennis was by far the quickest way to the poor house. I discovered that there was a great deal of over-reaction when certain events occur; and situations seemed to repeat themselves time and time again. It was then just a case of finding the ideal trading plan.

Tradeonsports

It was during this period that I became a Betfair accredited trainer. As an accredited Betfair trainer I am amazed by some of the queries and questions I receive and, indeed, by some of the characters I have spoken to. This has included someone who was blindly laying horses at 8/1 for £50 in the belief that they were going to win £400 if the horses lost.

It was then I decided to take the whole thing further by starting a service, *tradeonsports*. I started a newsletter which showed how the markets moved in various events over the previous month's sporting tournaments and matches. I analysed and back-tested this information to come up with various trading plans that can be used in the markets.

Lessons from the financial markets

There are many similarities between trading on Betfair and trading the financial markets, but it is my belief that the majority of Betfair customers are simply not aware of this. Disciplines learnt from the financial markets could improve their profit immensely. Indeed, although nothing can be guaranteed when entering a trade, I can say from experience that if you consistently follow the disciplines, strategies and rules that are highlighted in this book there is every chance that you will become a very successful sports trader.

As a Betfair accredited trainer I have met many people who are new to the concept of trading the sporting markets and are hungry for more information. I believe there is a gap in the market for a good book on the topic – I hope that this book will fill that gap.

It is my belief that trading on Betfair whilst watching live sport is one of the best hobbies you can have – and there is surely nothing better than having a hobby that can be both enjoyable and profitable!

A Brief History of Betfair

Betfair was launched in June 2000. The concept of person-to-person betting first came on the scene in the UK with the website Flutter.com in May 2000. Flutter was initially envisioned as an online betting community where the user would list the bets they would like to make and other users would then choose whether to accept the bet. Betfair on the other hand was built more like a stock exchange. Flutter soon realised that Betfair possessed the better approach to the market and altered its site to reflect this. After going head to head for a year, Flutter then decided to merge with Betfair in December 2001.

Controversy

Betfair's existence has not been without controversy. Now that punters can lay bets on all outcomes it has come in for criticism from the more traditional bookmakers. These bookmakers have argued that by allowing punters to bet that an outcome will not happen, this can result in causing corruption in sports such as horse racing, as it would be far easier to ensure that a horse will not win a race than to guarantee that it will win it. However, the exchange companies (like Betfair) would argue that whilst corruption in sport is possible, the major bookmakers are only really concerned with commercial interests rather than the integrity of sporting events.

Betfair have signed agreements with various governing bodies of sport (including the Jockey Club) with whom they have pledged to fully co-operate if the latter suspects that any corruption has taken place. Indeed, in the summer of 2004, Betfair provided data to various authorities which led to 16 arrests on charges relating to race fixing.

Rapid growth

In February 2006 Betfair launched a new interface which included in-play scores on football, tennis and cricket as well as highlighting jockey silks and form for horse racing.

In April 2006 SoftBank purchased 23% of Betfair, valuing the company at £1.5 billion; and in December of the same year Betfair completed the purchase of the horse racing company Timeform.

In March 2007 Betfair launched its own radio service which is broadcast from their headquarters in Hammersmith, London. This service is broadcast seven days a week and includes commentary on horse racing and greyhound racing as well as updated sports news and results.

Today, Betfair is the world's largest betting exchange with over one million customers and a turnover of over £50 million a week.

PART ONE

Getting started

1. Betting Basics

For those of you who are already reasonably experienced with Betfair, the following will be common knowledge and you may wish to skip on to Part Two.

For those reading this book who have no experience of betting or bookmakers, in the following few pages I am going to be dealing with some simple betting terminology. I will also explain how Betfair prices its odds and how a traditional bookmaker makes money.

I will also be explaining the commissioning charges and, briefly, the advantages of trading the in-play markets, as well as looking at placing a trade on Betfair.

A simple trade

When you log onto the Betfair site and start looking at a market you will be presented with a table highlighting the current available odds. In the example below we are going to look at a football match between Tottenham and Newcastle (Figure 1.1).

In a football match we are presented with six possible options. We can *back* or *lay* the Home win, the Away win or the Draw.

- If you **back** a team or individual, you are stating that you are expecting that this event **will** occur.

- If you **lay** a team or individual, you are saying this event will **not** occur.

In this particular case:

- If you were to **back** Tottenham you are expecting Tottenham to win.

- If you **lay** Tottenham you are saying that Newcastle will win the match or it will end up being a draw.

The best available prices are always displayed in the middle of the table. In the example below, the best odds available for Tottenham to win the match are currently 1.73.

However there is also money available at odds of 1.72 and 1.71. This money is from the punters who are laying the Tottenham win but do not want to accept the current price of 1.73.

Should someone back Tottenham at 1.73 with £866, the odds at 1.73 would disappear and be replaced by the next price in the queue (i.e. those people who have layed at the odds of 1.72).

Figure 1.1: Odds available Tottenham v Newcastle

Tottenham v Newcastle ⊞						
☐ Going in-play ☷ Live Scores				Matched: GBP 121,771 Refresh		
☑ Back & Lay ☑ Market Depth						More options ▶
Selections: (3)	100.4%		**Back**	**Lay**		99.5%
🏠 Tottenham	1.71 £748	1.72 £505	1.73 £866	1.74 £193	1.75 £2071	1.76 £233
🏠 Newcastle	5.7 £542	5.8 £162	5.9 £211	6 £340	6.2 £226	6.4 £675
🏠 The Draw	3.8 £1644	3.85 £422	3.9 £961	3.95 £253	4 £457	4.1 £951

On the lay side you will see that £193 is available to lay at 1.74, and the odds of 1.75 and 1.76 come from those who have backed Tottenham hoping to gain a better price than is currently available.

Backing

As you can see from the preceding table, there is £866 available to back Tottenham at the odds of 1.73.

If you were to back at the lower price of 1.72, your bet would automatically get filled at the higher price of 1.73, providing that the total monetary value of your bet is available.

One thing to remember is that Betfair *always* automatically matches your bet at the best available odds, whether you are backing or laying.

In this example, if you back Tottenham you are saying *I bet £100 that Tottenham will win this match and want to receive 1.73 times my stake.*

In this case, should Tottenham win, your return would be £173.

The 1.73 representing 1 + .73, the 1 being your stake of £100 and .73 being the £73 risk that the layer is putting up for you.

Just to clarify, should you want to back and ask for better odds than are currently available your bet will appear on the lay side of the market.

Laying

If you *lay* Tottenham, you are saying that Tottenham will not win the match. In other words, you are saying the game will result in either a:

- Newcastle win, or a
- draw.

If you were to lay Tottenham for £100 and they did not win, you would win £100.

However, should Tottenham win, then the odds of 1.74 represent your stake: 1 plus your risk of .74, which in this case would be £74.

So a Tottenham win would represent a loss of £74.

The unexpected happens

On the subject of laying, it is amazing the number of times that value can be found by laying at what would initially seem extremely low odds. It is at this lower end of the market that people really overestimate the chances of an event happening, and it is surprising how often the unexpected happens. Here are a few examples.

- Australia v England, Second Ashes test in Adelaide, December 2006. Going into the fifth day a draw looked a certainty priced at 1.05. That is until Shane Warne started reeling his magic and, following the usual England collapse, Australia cruised to an easy victory, and went 2-0 up in the series.

- Liverpool v AC Milan, European Champions League Final. This is a classic example. AC Milan were 3-0 up at half time and trading at 1.01. Liverpool then went on to make a comeback of historical proportions, and won the trophy on penalties. That night hundreds of thousands of pounds were traded and lost at 1.01.

- US Open 2006. Going down the final hole of this event both Phil Mickelson and Colin Montgomerie traded at under 1.50, with neither going on to be successful, as Geoff Ogilvy went on to win his first major.

Low laying opportunities happen all the time in sports such as golf, tennis and one-day cricket. And thanks to the in-play markets, the unexpected often happens; meaning that the odds can move significantly. We will explore some more examples of these in later chapters.

Betfair pricing

All prices quoted on Betfair are *decimal* odds. Decimal odds differ from the odds traditionally quoted in the UK in that they include your stake as part of your total return.

If you place a bet of £10 at decimal odds of 4.0 and win, then your total return (including stake) is £40.

In the UK this would traditionally be quoted as 3/1, returning to you winnings of £30 plus your original stake of £10.

Decimal odds are simpler to use than traditional odds, and are the most common form of odds quoted in countries outside the UK.

In addition, for the mathematically minded, decimal odds relate more closely to probability. For example, in a tennis match with two equally-matched players, the probability of each player winning is 50%. Each player will have traditional odds of 1/1 or decimal odds of 2.0. Hence, the probability of an outcome equals 1 divided by its decimal odds (1/2.0 = 50%).

Decimal odds also offer many more incremental prices – Betfair offer every price between 1.01 and 2.0, to two decimal places.

Converting decimal odds to traditional odds

Decimal odds minus 1.0 = traditional odds (x to 1)

For example, 4.0 = 3/1, 1.80 = 4/5 (0.8 to 1)

Converting traditional odds to decimal odds

Traditional odds (x to 1) plus 1.0 = decimal odds

For example, 7/1 = 8.0, 1/2 = 1.50

Betfair odds conversion chart

Fractional	Decimal	Fractional	Decimal
10/1	11.00	8/13	1.62
9/1	10.00	4/7	1.57
8/1	9.00	8/15	1.53
7/1	8.00	½	1.50
6/1	7.00	4/9	1.44
5/1	6.00	2/5	1.40
4/1	5.00	4/11	1.36
3/1	4.00	1/3	1.33
2/1	3.00	2/7	1.29
Evs	2.00	¼	1.25
10/11	1.91	2/9	1.22
5/6	1.83	1/5	1.20
4/5	1.80	1/6	1.17
8/11	1.73	1/7	1.14
4/6	1.67	1/8	1.13

Probability

If you look at any market on Betfair you will see two percentage figures in the back and lay column. Using the Tottenham v Newcastle game as an example, on the back side it is 100.4% and on the lay side it is 99.5%.

This figure should add up to near 100%, as we know that there are only three possible outcomes: a Tottenham win, a Newcastle win or a draw

Each of the odds represents the implied probability that the event will occur. We can work out the implied probability by dividing 100 by the odds on offer (as shown in the following table).

Event	Price	100/Price	Percentage
Tottenham win	1.73	100/1.73	57.80%
Newcastle win	5.9	100/5.9	16.94%
Draw	3.9	100/3.9	25.64%
TOTAL			100.38%

In the example above, the market is telling us that Tottenham have a 57.80% chance of winning this match. Odds compilers calculate these probability figures fairly accurately and over a period of time you would generally find that the odds on offer match the results that occur.

Betting terminology

Odds and prices

Throughout the book you will come across the terms *price* and *odds*. For example,

'*Liverpool's odds are 2.5 to beat Manchester United*' or

'*The price for Liverpool to beat Manchester United is 2.5*'

These two are the same thing and throughout the book the terms are used interchangeably.

Shortening and drifting

You will come across terms such as –

'*The price has shortened from 3.0 to 2.5*'

Shortened means that the price has fallen or the percentage chance of an event happening has increased.

When the price *drifts* it means that the odds have increased, for example from 2.5 to 3.0. This then has the effect that the percentage chance of this event happening has decreased.

How does a bookmaker make money?

A bookmaker takes money from the bets placed by customers, pays out the winners and keeps the money of losers. It's a quite a simple concept. However, this doesn't explain how a bookmaker can make money in the long run.

The over round

When a bookmaker sets the odds, he builds what is known as an 'over round' into the odds. This over round is sometimes also known as 'juice'.

For example, in a cricket Twenty20 World Cup final, there are two finalists – India and Pakistan. And in this example we are assuming that both have an equal chance (50%) of winning. Fair odds for this event would then be even money (or, in decimal, 2.0). So if you were to place £10 on India, and India win, you win £10 and get your £10 back.

However, a traditional bookmaker would not offer even money.

They might offer 5/6 (1.83) on both India and Pakistan. So your £10 would only return £8.30 plus your stake.

1.83 equates to a 54.6% chance of winning.

So the bookmaker in this example has stated that India have a 54.6% chance of winning and Pakistan also have a 54.6% chance of winning. If we add both of the 54.6% chances together we come up with 109%, so the book value is 109% in this example.

And this 9% is known as the bookmaker's *over round*.

You can see that if the bookmaker has an equal amount of money on both teams, the bookmaker will win regardless of the outcome.

For example, if they took £5000 on India and £5000 on Pakistan, they would then take £5000 from the loser but only have to pay out £4150 on the winner, making a profit of £850 regardless.

Betfair operates differently from traditional bookmakers, in that Betfair does not make prices. Instead they are an exchange, where customers make and take prices themselves. Betfair then makes money by charging commission on trades.

Betfair commission

Betfair charge a commission on your net winnings, so you only pay commission if you have a winning trade. If you have a net loss on a market, you do not pay commission.

Commission is calculated by multiplying your net winnings by the *Market Base Rate*. A win of £100 on a market with a Market Base Rate of 5% would result in you paying £5 in commission.

To find the Market Base Rate you go to the Rules tab of the market you are trading (Figure 1.2).

Commission is generally charged at 5%.

Figure 1.2: Market Base Rate Commission

Premium commission charges

Since the writing of this book began, Betfair have introduced *Premium Charges* (which they claim will affect less than 0.5% of their most successful customers).

Looking at the conditions, they seem overly complicated – and definitely aimed at the successful horse racing trader. The following is taken from the Betfair site:

Premium charge summary

You will only be considered for the Premium Charge if, over the previous 60 weeks, you satisfy the following criteria:

- Your account is in profit;

- Your total charges generated are less than 20% of gross profits; and

- You bet in more than 250 markets.

Two further conditions reduce the likelihood that you will be required to pay the Premium Charge:

- Any single win that constitutes more than 50% of your gross profits over the previous 60 weeks will be excluded from the calculation; and

- Each customer will have a 60 week allowance of £1000 against the Premium Charge.

Each week the customers who meet all the conditions set out above will be charged the lesser of:

- The difference between 20% of the previous week's gross profits and the total charges generated during the week; and

- The difference between 20% of the previous 60 weeks' gross profits and the total charges generated during that period.

Obviously the above is concerning for those whose only source of income comes from the Betfair markets. For the rest, I would not be too worried. However, it is not good news if these big traders no longer participate in the markets, as a substantial amount of liquidity could disappear. I think this a situation that will obviously be monitored over time and it will be interesting to see if this charge makes any difference to the liquidity and customer base of Betfair's biggest rival Betdaq.

The benefits of in-play trading

So far we have explored a number of the opportunities available to punters on Betfair. We can get excellent prices on backing an event, as the over round is nearly always close to 0% as opposed to the bookmakers' normal over round of around 10%. Also, if we don't like the prices on offer we can ask for better odds. However, the real advantage of using Betfair arises when trading an event.

The benefits of in-play trading are best illustrated in a live sporting event. Let's look at the example of an Indian Premier League cricket match between Bangalore and Rajasthan.

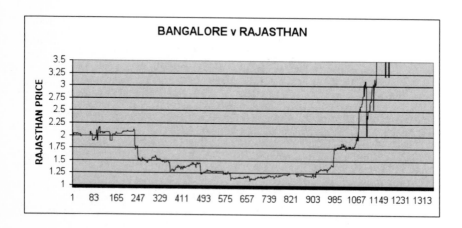

Rajasthan started the match at a price of 2.0.

They grabbed a quick couple of wickets and their price quickly dropped to 1.50.

Bangalore wickets continued to fall steadily and they finished the innings on 133 for 8. Rajasthan were then hot favourites, trading at 1.13 before coming in to bat.

Rajasthan started their innings and lost a couple of quick wickets, and at 7 for 2 they then traded at 1.75.

Rajasthan continued to lose wickets and were bowled out for 58, going on to lose the match.

Now it is very easy to be wise after the event, but imagine the position you could have put yourself in if you believed Bangalore were protecting a decent total.

Laying Rajasthan at 1.13 wouldn't exactly break the bank. For the potential profit of £100, your risk would have been £13. You have to ask yourself –

What is the downside of such a lay?

The worst that could have happened is Rajasthan rattle off 40 runs in 5 overs, and even then you could trade out for a loss at around 1.05.

In this case, at any point after the first two overs, you had a healthy position to trade from.

Trading price movement

Today many traders are not making a judgement on the final result of an event but are trading the movements of the odds price.

Odds can move dramatically in any in-play market or sporting event, as seen by the previous example. However, it is also possible to capture significant price movements before an event has even started.

 The key to a successful trade is that you must always Lay under your Back.

As an example, you are looking at a Test match cricket market between England and Australia and you notice that due to a poor long range weather forecast there is the possibility of a couple of lost days' play. The price for the Draw has now moved down from 2.7 to 2.5 and you believe the price will fall even further.

You then decide to place a:

> £50 *back* bet on the Draw at 2.5 which would leave you with a potential £75 profit (£50 x 1.5).

Should the Draw price go down to 2.2 you can then *lay* for the same amount (£50) which would then leave you with a potential £60 liability (£50 x 1.2).

This ensures that you have netted a profit of £15 should the match indeed end up being a Draw.

This £15 is the difference between the £75 potential profit when backed at 2.5 and the £60 potential liability when laying the Draw at 2.2.

Your potential loss on both England and Australia is zero, so you cannot lose on this match. This is summarised in the following table.

	Bet #1 (£50 back bet on the Draw at 2.5)	Bet #2 (£50 lay bet on the Draw at 2.2)	Net profit
England win	-50	50	0
Australia win	-50	50	0
Draw	75	-60	15

Conversely, should you have backed the Draw for £50 at 2.5, and it then drifted out to 2.8 and you layed for the same amount, you would be facing a £15 loss.

However, only if the match ends up being a draw would the loss materialise. If the match ends up being a victory for England or Australia you end up losing nothing.

There are many traders in the market who have practised this until it is a fine art, and they can gain a profit up to 90% with careful timing of the trade they place.

In reality, though, just about any sports event can be traded. The only knowledge you require is how and why the odds move, and we shall be looking more at this topic later.

One major advantage of trading is that, should you be in a position where you have secured a profit, you can then transfer that money back into the market on the other selections. This ensures that you make a profit no matter who wins, and is called *greening up*. I shall be dealing with it in the next section.

Greening up

Greening up is the term used for equalising your profit across an event, regardless of outcome. (It is known as 'greening up' because green is the colour of the font Betfair uses to indicate if your selection is in profit.)

To demonstrate an example of this we shall have a look at the following scenario.

> *Note*: The following scenario is just an example to show the greening-up process. The trading process in this example is high risk and not advisable for the novice trader.

We are watching a football match between Fulham and West Ham.

Just before kick-off the following prices are available (Figure 1.3).

Figure 1.3: Odds available for Fulham v West Ham match

	BACK	LAY
FULHAM	2.24 £2025	2.26 £3216
WEST HAM	3.60 £1267	3.65 £1687
DRAW	3.60 £326	3.65 £558

Fulham have started the match very brightly. They have been on the attack constantly and have come very close to scoring on at least two occasions.

> *Note*: Although Fulham have started the match well they have not scored a goal and so their price has risen.

Around the 20-minute mark the match prices look like this (Figure 1.4).

Figure 1.4: Odds for Fulham v West Ham match 0-0 after 20 minutes of play

	BACK	LAY
FULHAM	2.38 £920	2.40 £354
WEST HAM	3.70 £256	3.75 £2096
DRAW	3.20 £2033	3.25 £800

At this stage, as Fulham have started so well and look like scoring, we do the following –

Back Fulham with £100 at 2.38 hoping that they will score a goal, take the lead and go on to win the match.

So our current profit/loss scenario is –

1. If Fulham win we will win £138.

2. If the game is a draw or West Ham win we will lose our stake of £100.

As you will see from Figure 1.5 after placing the trade, in the first column the profit and loss is shown underneath each outcome.

So in this example Fulham are +£138.00, West Ham are -£100.00 and the draw is -£100.00

Figure 1.5: Potential profit and loss after placing £100 Back bet on Fulham at 2.38

	BACK	LAY
FULHAM +£138.00	2.38 £920	2.40 £354
WEST HAM -£100.00	3.70 £256	3.75 £2096
DRAW -£100.00	3.20 £2033	3.25 £800

Shortly after making our bet, Fulham score and the odds on them winning now shoot down to 1.40 (Figure 1.6).

Figure 1.6: Match odds after Fulham take 1–0 lead

	BACK	LAY
FULHAM +£138.00	1.40 £49	1.41 £208
WEST HAM -£100.00	10.50 £1428	11.00 £2096
DRAW -£100.00	5.20 £195	5.30 £36

Firstly, we shall take a look at how the odds have moved.

Fulham started the game at 2.24 (44.64% chance of winning). The first 20 minutes were goalless, and Fulham's price drifted to 2.38 (42.01% chance of winning). Fulham then scored. At this stage the market was suspended (i.e. the market closed).

Note: The market is always suspended after a goal is scored in football. The market is generally closed for up to a minute.

When the market reopens we see that Fulham's odds have shortened to 1.40 (71.42% chance of winning).

It is at this time that we have the following choices –

1. *We can decide to let the bet run*
   If we let the bet run we will win £138.00 if Fulham win. However, if West Ham equalise or go onto win, we would then lose £100.

2. *We can lay Fulham*
   If we now lay Fulham for £100 we are locking in an immediate profit.

In the following table you can see that by backing Fulham for £100 at 2.38 and then laying them for £100 at 1.41 (and thus losing £41 should Fulham go on to win) we have created a risk-free gain of £97 (which equates to our initial profit of £138 - £41 = £97) if Fulham go onto win the match. The profit/loss scenario now is shown in the following table–

	Bet #1 (Back Fulham for £100 at 2.38)	Bet #2 (Lay Fulham for £100 at 1.41)	Net profit
Fulham win	138	-41	97
West Ham win	-100	100	0
Draw	-100	100	0

So, Fulham are currently winning (1-0) and if the game stays like this then we stand to win £97. However, should West Ham score an equaliser in the final few minutes (and the game is a draw) then we will lose the £97 profit (gained by previously backing and laying Fulham) and merely come out evens (no profit or loss). See Figure 1.7.

Figure 1.7: Profit and loss after backing Fulham for £100 at 2.38 and laying Fulham for £100 at 1.40

	BACK	LAY
FULHAM +£97.00	1.40 £49	1.41 £208
WEST HAM £0.00	10.50 £1428	11.00 £2096
DRAW £0.00	5.20 £195	5.30 £36

But a third option exists. *We can green up: equalising our profits on the match – regardless of the outcome.*

With this option we take out all the risk and guarantee a profit, no matter what the final result of the match is. This is done as follows.

We currently have £97 for Fulham to win and a zero outcome on the draw or the West Ham win.

With the £97 profit we do a quick calculation –

The money that is currently available on the Fulham win is divided by Fulham's current lay odds (1.41).

```
£97/1.41 = £68.79
```

So by laying Fulham for £68.79 at 1.41, we are guaranteeing that no matter what the result in this match we will win £68.79. This can be explained as follows –

- the current profit on Fulham is £97 and there is £0.00 on both the draw and West Ham,

- the current lay price for Fulham is 1.41,

- we then divide the money that is currently available on Fulham, which is £97, and divide it by the Fulham lay price of 1.41,

- £97 divided by 1.41 = £68.79,

- we are then laying Fulham for £68.79 (this means we are saying 'not Fulham'),

- so if Fulham win we will be £68.79 in profit; which equals the initial profit of £97 minus £28.21, which is the liability of laying Fulham for £68.79 at 1.41.

- If the game is a West Ham win we will be £68.79 in profit as £68.79 is the amount we layed by saying not Fulham.

- If the game is a draw we will be £68.79 in profit as £68.79 is the amount we layed by saying not Fulham.

- So we win £68.79 no matter if the result is a Fulham win, a West Ham win, or a draw (See Figure 1.8).

This is summarised in the following table.

	Bet #1 (Back Fulham for £100 at 2.38)	Bet #2 (Lay Fulham for £100 at 1.41)	Bet #3 (Lay Fulham for £97 at 1.41)	Net profit
Fulham win	138	–41	–28.21	68.79
West Ham win	–100	100	68.79	68.79
Draw	–100	100	68.79	68.79

Note: In theory we could both back the draw and the West Ham win which is the same as laying Fulham, but the calculations are far more complicated and it is much easier to just to carry out one transaction.

Figure 1.8: £68.79 profit after greening up

	BACK	LAY
FULHAM +£68.79	1.40 £49	1.41 £208
WEST HAM +£68.79	10.50 £1428	11.00 £2096
DRAW +£68.79	5.20 £195	5.30 £36

Obviously we have had to sacrifice nearly £30 of profit to ensure that we win whatever the result, but at least now we no longer have to concern ourselves with the result: a guaranteed profit of £68.79 has now been secured *whatever the outcome*.

Note: Once again I must stress that the scenario above is just to highlight how to 'green up' in an *in–play market*. This example is high risk and not advisable for the novice trader.

Using the more options tab to help create an 'all green' book

The above may at first seem complicated. However, fortunately you can set up your Betfair account to make the process very simple.

For example, if we look at the Man Utd v Chelsea market (Figure 1.9) we will see there is a 'More options' link.

Figure 1.9: Man Utd v Chelsea 'More options' link

Betfair Soccer » Man Utd v Chelsea							
Man Utd v Chelsea ⊕					Matched: GBP 83,436	Refresh	
☐ Going in-play 📷 Live Scores							
☑ Back & Lay ☑ Market Depth						More options ▸	
Selections: (3)	100.5%		**Back**	**Lay**		99.2%	
📊 **Man Utd**	3.1 £2981	3.15 £1933	3.2 £2583	3.25 £3031	3.3 £1406	3.35 £1694	
📊 **Chelsea**	2.56 £2162	2.58 £1671	2.6 £3770	2.62 £308	2.64 £8314	2.66 £93	
📊 **The Draw**	3.15 £6664	3.2 £7066	3.25 £8633	3.3 £2087	3.35 £13364	3.4 £4623	

On clicking this link you will be presented with various options (Figure 1.10). Ensure that you tick the 'Show Profit and Loss' and 'Display "what if" figure'.

Figure 1.10: More options dialogue box

Say you decide to see what would happen if you wanted to place £100 on Man Utd. You go into the Place Bets box and look to back Man Utd for £100 (Figure 1.11).

> *Note:* Remember you are not placing a bet, you are just seeing what the outcome of placing a bet would be.

Figure 1.11: Placing £100 bet on Man Utd

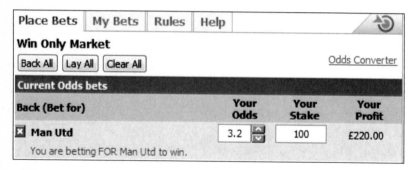

The following figure shows the profit and loss for all outcomes.

Figure 1.12: the potential profit and loss highlighted

Man Utd v Chelsea ⊞						Matched: GBP 85,191 Refresh	
☐ Going in-play ⊞ Live Scores							
☑ Back & Lay ☑ Market Depth						More options ▸	
Selections: (3)	100.5%		Back	Lay		99.2%	
Man Utd » £220.00	3.1 £3015	3.15 £1899	3.2 £2560	3.25 £2685	3.3 £1406	3.35 £1700	
Chelsea » -£100.00	2.56 £2143	2.58 £1671	2.6 £3356	2.62 £268	2.64 £8286	2.66 £93	
The Draw » -£100.00	3.15 £6664	3.2 £7051	3.25 £8288	3.3 £2087	3.35 £13342	3.4 £4496	

As can be seen, the profit and loss profile is –

- Man Utd win: £220.00 in green (which shows you are in profit)

- Chelsea win: £100 in red (which highlights a loss)

- Draw: £100 in red (which highlights a loss)

So in this example if we place £100 on Man Utd at 3.20 we would be in a position of winning £220 should Man Utd win, or losing £100 should Chelsea win or the match end in a draw.

Now we shall take a look (Figure 1.13) at what would happen should we then decide to lay Man United for £105 at 3.0, after previously backing them for £100 at 3.20.

Figure 1.13: Placing further lay bet of £100 on Man Utd

We can now see by looking at Figure 1.14 what effect backing Man Utd for £100 at 3.2 and then laying Man Utd for £105 at 3.0 will have on your profit and loss.

Figure 1.14: the potential profit and an 'all green' book highlighted

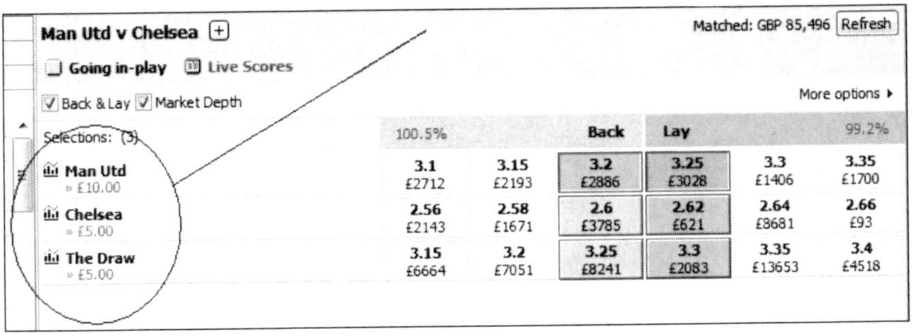

As can be seen, the profit and loss profile is –

- Man Utd win: £10.00 in green (which shows you are in profit)

- Chelsea win: £5.00 in green (which shows you are in profit)

- Draw: £5.00 in green (which shows you are in profit)

So we have now created an all green book, which means we have profited no matter what the result.

This function should always be switched on as it avoids much confusion.

2. Hardware and Software Requirements

Connection

To participate in these markets, a decent PC with a broadband internet connection is essential.

Also as you may at times be committing considerable sums of money into the market, it is recommended that in case you lose internet connection you have a landline and mobile phone close by. You should have the following to hand and available at all times, as well –

- The **Betfair phone number:** 0844 871 5555 (UK), +44 20 8834 8060 (from non-UK).

- Your **telephone account number** (which can be located under 'My Account' on the home page and under 'My Profile').

A couple of years ago on the Saturday evening before the last round of the British Open, I decided to lay Tiger Woods for £500 at around 1.94. I was hoping that, should someone emerge from the pack early during the final round, his price would drift out.

Indeed the price did start moving out to 2.18 a couple of hours before he was due to tee off. It was at this time I decided to log on and take the profit. Except I could not log on to the internet, as my service provider was unavailable.

I quickly realised that not only did I not have the Betfair telephone number, but I also did not have my account number. I was lucky that day, I was eventually able to exit the trade when connection returned.

However, a valuable lesson had certainly been learnt.

Always ensure you keep the Betfair phone number and your telephone account number to hand.

Costs

Trading seriously on Betfair does not come cheap. However, given the fact that most homes now have internet and satellite TV, some of the below can be discounted as already belonging in the household budget. Here is a typical breakdown of essential monthly costs –

- Internet (£18)
- Sky Sports (£42)
- API Bet Angel (£15)

Approx monthly outgoing: £75.

Live TV feed and in-play markets

When trading certain sports I generally ensure that I have access to the live pictures. This should speak for itself, but it is surprising the number of people who trade blind on most sports. Even if this means paying for an additional Sky/cable box, it will save you money in the long term.

Also always make sure that when an event is advertised as in-play, it is broadcast on one of the readily available satellite channels.

Although this happens rarely these days, as all Premiership matches are now available to trade in-play, I placed a position in a recent Fulham v Bolton match that was advertised as in-play and it turned out that it wasn't. I scoured through the various radio listings but could find no advertised broadcasting of this event.

The match started, and the market closed. I complained to Betfair but they said that they could change this rule at any time, and as the match was not broadcast on any mainstream media it was impossible for them to monitor. Thus they could not turn the market in-play. I was fortunate in this case as they reopened the market at half-time; the game was goalless and I was able to trade out for a profit.

 Always ensure that an event is broadcast on satellite TV before committing any money.

PART TWO

The Trading Process

3. The Learning Process

Now that we have covered the basics of trading on the Betfair site we are now going to go through the processes necessary for you to become a competent trader.

Unfortunately, there is no shortcut to becoming proficient on Betfair. Many people believe that they have suddenly become an expert just because they have had the odd winning trade.

Professionals and tradesmen all have to go through various forms of education and apprenticeship before ever getting near being able to operate competently, so why should trading on the betting exchanges be any different?

To get the skills and results you desire is going to take time, effort and dedication. You will not become an expert sports trader by simply reading a couple of books or attending the odd seminar; you are going to have to put in the time and effort in order to be successful.

The Three Learning Phases

There are three major stages to becoming an expert –

Stage 1 – The untrained trader

Initially you should concentrate on learning how to use the Betfair site and preserve your trading capital. It is during this initial period when mistakes and losses are inevitable. At this stage the new sports trader should not get discouraged as every losing trade presents an opportunity to learn and ensure that the mistake is *not* repeated.

Any worthwhile skill takes time to learn and in the first few months your trading bank (i.e. the money you have set aside to bet with) should be looked upon more as training fees rather than trading capital. It is also critical not to go mad from the start by risking large sums of capital on only a few trades; large early losses will only breed discouragement – and large early wins will only breed over-confidence!

This should be a period of learning and fun; as you should be trading with minimum stakes, your confidence should be growing all the time.

Experience as many markets as possible

It is also during this period that you should expose yourself to as many markets as possible, to see which markets you are comfortable with, and to find your true trading style.

You may very well be surprised and find that your specialisation lies within a sport you previously thought you had no real affinity towards. Personally I have always loved watching football and golf, but since studying the Betfair markets I have renewed my enthusiasm for cricket and developed a real interest in American football.

Use this initial period to experiment fully and you may be surprised at what comes up.

Stage 2 – The competent trader

It is at this stage where the sports trader has found the markets in which he is interested, and is now dedicating more time to learning the techniques needed to be successful.

It is also the period when the trader realises that his skills are above average compared with the majority of traders; I believe that most traders reading this book would be very happy to reach this stage.

It is very difficult to put a timeline on when a trader could hope to reach the competent stage, but I would suggest that if you are prepared to commit yourself to the disciplines mentioned in this book there is no reason why this cannot be achieved within two to three years.

Stage 3 – The expert trader

This is the stage where the trading becomes a real focus in life. The trader becomes immersed in his subject, and a large proportion of time is involved in the specific study of one or two markets. The goal here is excellence and very few people go on to attain this status.

Characteristics of the successful trader

To become an expert on Betfair I believe you need to posses the following characteristics; indeed, ultimately, everything is measured in your level of commitment to the three points highlighted below.

1. Having a great passion for the subject.

2. Wanting to be the best trader you can.

3. The willingness to be disciplined enough to put in the time and effort required to become an expert.

To begin with you must have a strong interest in the subject of sport and trading and be willing and disciplined enough to commit to your goals.

Many traders will have found their own niche, and created their own trading system from which they are making a nice sum of money. This is because they have a passion and love for the subject.

If you are doing this just for the financial reward, it will inevitably be reflected in your results.

The trader's journey

To summarise, you should view the learning process and your trading career as a continuous journey towards expertise. You must be patient and give yourself the necessary time to develop and improve your skills and your goal should be that of ever improving.

By following the processes as outlined in this book you should find that your techniques, skills and profits are increasing and improving on a yearly basis.

To help you on your way I have devised a series of 18 rules that, if followed, should enable you to become a profitable trader. They will appear at the end of each relevant section. Here is the first one.

Rule 1: Experience as many markets as possible

When opening an account and starting on Betfair, expose yourself to as many markets as possible to see which sports are best suited to your individual trading style.

4. Having Attainable Goals

You have now looked at all the markets available to trade on Betfair, and have committed yourself to being the best trader you can be.

You start dreaming of all the things you are going to buy and what you are going to spend all that extra money on.

It is now that you need to have a reality check and set yourself some realistic and attainable goals. This process is vital if you are to succeed on Betfair.

Winning can be bad

As bizarre as it may sound, the worst thing that can happen to an inexperienced trader is to have a very good winning start. If a new trader who has an initial bank of £1000 gets off to a great start and wins £100 in a day, they may then expect to win this amount every day.

This then leads to unrealistic expectations. It also leads to chasing losses, overtrading and taking on far too much risk. Indeed, winning £100 a day with a bank of £1000 is far too unrealistic; and yet you would be amazed at how many new traders find these figures to be genuinely achievable.

For example, it is far easier for a trader to win £100 a day if he has a capital of £10,000, than it would be for someone who only has a bank of £1000. Even then, for the trader with the bank of £10,000, £100 a day would be very difficult to obtain on a consistent day-to-day basis.

Set realistic goals

It is far better to set small and achievable goals, so that they keep you on the right track whilst your trading bank grows steadily and proportionately.

As you can see in the Appendix, in a month I made 97 trades on tennis whilst risking £50 a trade. The system then went on to profit by £631.55, showing a return of just over 13% (an overall profit of £6.51 a trade).

The above is a good example of realistic goal setting as the target profit is linked in correct proportion to the capital available.

A trader will obviously experience losing days and days when not much happens in the market, but traders should remember that goals are, essentially, guidelines to help you towards the overall profit, and do not need to be achieved every single day.

Case study

Unrealistic goal setting and the pressure that comes from using trading as a primary source of income can cause an individual to make some very bad decisions.

I visited a client recently who wanted me to teach his son how to trade the Betfair markets. His aspiration was for his son to make more money trading on Betfair than getting a job during the summer holidays. I joked that maybe his son should be teaching me how to trade!

The ten weeks his son was dedicating to the markets would certainly be a valuable learning curve, but I did feel that he was putting his son under intense pressure because as soon as real money is involved everything *can* and *does* go wrong.

I felt that in his eagerness to achieve an over-ambitious daily profit, discipline could go out of the window, and that by chasing unrealistic targets, a single loss could wipe out all previously made profits, and more.

I also pointed out to him that if his son were to follow a set trading plan, there could be long periods of time when there were no markets available to trade because of the criteria he had set. This would then cause his son to go looking for risky trades elsewhere.

I spoke to the father a few weeks later to find out how his son had got on over the holidays and he informed me that after four weeks his son had gone out to work, as he had been completely discouraged by a couple of large losses.

I expressed my disappointment and stated that this situation could easily have been avoided if his son had been given a reasonable, no-pressure learning period, combined with realistic goals.

You can avoid the above experience of discouragement by following this rule.

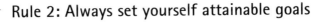

Rule 2: Always set yourself attainable goals

Set yourself a realistic time frame to learn and become competent on the Betfair markets. Also set yourself realistic financial goals that are proportionate to your trading bank.

5. Your Trading Bank

You have now decided the markets you like to trade and have set yourself some realistic goals. Now you need to seriously think about how much money you should put aside to trade with.

The subject of trading capital is difficult to approach, as everyone is working from a different amount of available capital that they have at their disposal.

The beauty of Betfair is that with the £2 minimum stake, everyone should be able to afford to start at some level. If you are a beginner I would say it is quite adequate to start with a deposit of £50-£200.

The rules of capitalisation

The rules I would have for capitalisation are the following:

1. **Never play with previously allocated or borrowed money, and only trade with money you can afford to lose.**

   Once you start trading with money that is already allocated for a purpose, then your mind will start to do strange things. Ultimately you will begin losing discipline and start making illogical trading decisions. Never *ever* borrow money in order to fund your trading, as this then puts you under immediate pressure to start showing a return. Trading is hard enough without adding further stresses and problems.

2. **Only commit the amount of money that you are comfortable with.**

   This will allow you to perform to the best of your ability, as the inevitable loss can and will have an adverse effect on your confidence.

Trading in fear

When I place my money in the market I know that I can afford to lose the money that I am trading and that I am placing my money on a calculated risk. If my trades are successful I enjoy the rewards; but, if not, I put it down to experience, review my trading plan and move on.

Because I am trading with money that I can afford to lose my mindset is always the same. Whereas if you are trading with money that you can't afford to lose, it is almost certain that you will become a bad trader.

Trading with money you cannot afford to lose creates a sense of fear, which means that you do not execute your trades or follow your plans correctly. When under this type of pressure, the trader tends to gamble his way out of mistakes and fails to implement his stop losses. He starts to panic and then begins placing huge amounts of money on very short-priced favourites in order to get his money back.

Once gripped by fear, trading can become completely erratic, often by not letting trades hit the stop loss or cutting the winners short. By doing this the frequency of losing trades increases, and this then offsets any advantages gained from initially using a well thought out system.

Starting small

If you do not have a large amount of capital you have to face the fact that you are going to have to start small and build up your bank slowly – and keep your risks in line with your account size.

Building your capital slowly does not mean that you do not still follow rigid money management plans as you would with a larger trading bank. This is often forgotten by small stake traders, as they perceive that if they lose their entire bank then it is no big deal.

The reality is that in order to be successful you have to treat your small bank exactly the same as if you were adequately capitalised to make a living from trading. Your focus at this stage should be to simply become the best trader you can be.

Remember, if you are a bad trader with a £100 bank, you will still be a bad trader with a £10,000 bank. Once you master this, the money will follow.

The serious trader

Once your confidence has increased, so can your stakes. If you are looking to take trading on Betfair seriously I believe you need a bank of around £5000 – £10,000, assuming you are going to risk 1 to 2% on every trade.

Also if you intend to start employing strategies that scalp the market then you are going to need enough capital to make it all worthwhile.

If you are working with a bank of around £5000 – £10,000, then listed below are a number of suggestions –

1. **Do not keep all this money in your Betfair account,** as it is not earning any interest. Money can be moved very easily from your bank account to Betfair and vice versa, so there should be no reason to leave large sums of money in your account.

2. Always **plan ahead**, look forward and think about the actual capital you are going to need to trade the following day or so, and only have that amount of money available in your Betfair account. I often come across cases where people trade out of boredom, purely and simply because the money is available to use.

3. I use a **separate bank account** to fund my trading activities, and I would advise any serious trader to do likewise. You then know exactly where you stand at all times and it also places your trading on a more business-like level.

Stake size

It is imperative before you begin trading on Betfair to have a staking strategy, as large amounts of money can soon be lost if a trade goes against you.

For example, should you place £100 on an event at 4.40 and the odds move up to 4.90 you have effectively lost 50% of your stake. (Back £100 at 4.40 = possible profit £340 then lay £100 at 4.90 = possible liability £390; equates to £50 loss if this selection goes on to win.)

To combat this problem I stake in proportion to the implied probability, which involves staking my bank in accordance to tick size.

For example, if you are trading an event and the price is 1.57, Betfair will automatically increase or decrease the odds by .01. In this example, if the price fell by one tick it would be 1.56, and if it rose by one tick it would be 1.58.

If the event were priced at 2.56, the minimum tick increment would be .02. So if the odds fell by one tick it would be 2.54, or if it rose by one tick it would be 2.58; and if you traded an event at 3.50 the increase/decrease would be .05 and again the odds in this example would either be 3.45 or 3.55.

Betfair tick size for different ranges of prices

Tick size increment	Odds from	Odds to
0.01	1.01	2.00
0.02	2.02	3.00
0.05	3.05	4.00
0.1	4.10	6.00
0.2	6.20	10.00
0.5	10.50	20.00
1	21.00	30.00
2	32.00	50.00
5	55.00	100.00
10	110.00	1000.00

Using the table and example above you can see that if you placed £100 on a trade at 11.0 your stake would be wiped out in 2 ticks (2 x 0.5 of £100) should the odds drift up to 12.0.

Therefore the best way of approaching your stake size is to aim for a return per tick.

In the following table I have allocated £1 per tick, and thus should an event I wish to trade be priced at 5.0 I will automatically use a £10 stake.

Stake amounts governed by tick size

Staking at £1 a tick	Increment	Odds from	Odds to
£100	1%	1.01	2.00
£50	2%	2.02	3.00
£20	5%	3.05	4.00
£10	10%	4.10	6.00
£5	20%	6.20	10.00
£2	50%	10.50	20.00
£1	100%	21.00	30.00
£0.50	200%	32.00	50.00
£0.20	500%	55.00	100.00
£0.10	1000%	110.00	1000.00

By utilising this policy you are equalising your risk dependent on the odds/probability of the event happening.

How much you are risking per tick

When using tick sizes as your staking policy, and if you are trading at very low odds (i.e. under 2.0), it can seem that you are risking a huge amount of money. However, you should do your very best to try and ignore this issue and concentrate on how much you are risking per tick.

For example, should you back a selection for £200 at 1.68 and the odds go down to 1.63 or 5 ticks and you lay £200, at 1.63 you have effectively locked in £10 profit on this. You could also set a stop loss at 1.73, (again 5 ticks) and if the odds were to rise to this level you would be facing a possible £10 loss.

When you begin trading on Betfair, the easiest way of staking in the above way is by using the Bet Angel software (discussed at the end of this book). The software has a function that automatically alters your stake in line with the prices on offer. You do, however, need to be careful when the prices cross over from 1.99 to 2.02 or 2.98 to 3.05, etc, but otherwise this facility is excellent and extremely easy to set-up.

Rule 3: Only trade with money you can afford to lose

Never play with previously allocated or borrowed money and only trade with money you can afford to lose. You should also only commit the amount of money that you are comfortable with; this will allow you to perform to the best of your ability.

6. Paper and Minimum Stake Trading

Paper trading

Many people are divided on whether paper trading is a good idea or not.

For those who are not familiar with the term, *paper trading* is trading without using money. This is the only way to learn to trade without losing real money.

I believe it is a good idea. It would be very unwise to try a new system with a gung-ho approach, risking a large proportion of your capital without testing to find out if it is going to be profitable beforehand.

The downside of paper trading is that it does not give you that trading-with-real-money experience. When your hard-earned money is on the line, everything changes – as the emotional rollercoaster and mind games begin.

However, one of the major advantages and beauties of trading on Betfair is that the minimum amount of money you can risk on any one single trade is £2, this acts as a good halfway house between paper and real trading.

Test your system with the minimum stake

£2 is the minimal amount and, for a new or any other trader who is looking to test a system using paper trading, I would suggest using this minimum stake. Indeed, I would suggest that this is the best way to get you into the habit of playing with real money.

In part Five of this book I highlight a number of the strategies I use and, even though you may end up trading these systems that have already been proved and back-tested, I would still suggest that you test the trading system with minimum stakes for around three months.

Once you are happy that the system works, then and only then should you start increasing your stakes proportionally in line with your confidence, before using your normal staking plan.

Testing your emotions

To summarise, rather than paper trade, start trading with the minimum £2 stake; this has many advantages in that it will test your emotions, discipline and your ability to follow a rigid set of rules.

You can see if a trading system suits your personality or interest. It is also a sensible way for you to discover your trading niche. More importantly it gets you used to using real money, something that paper trading will never do.

Rule 4: When testing a system trade with the minimum stakes

When testing a new trading system, test the system with the minimum stakes before committing large sums of your trading capital.

7. Learning From Mistakes

One thing that is certain when you start trading on Betfair is that you will make mistakes. It is human nature. And even after having traded for some time, you are likely have the odd relapse or two. During my Betfair trading career I have made a number of costly mistakes. I give three examples below.

Example mistake #1

Crewe were playing at home against Manchester United in a Carling Cup game.

At this stage of my trading career I had not examined many markets. However, I had studied a little football and was becoming relatively successful at trading on the Under 2.5 goal market. I had built up a reasonable bank from £500 to around £1500 and my confidence was pretty high.

Anyway, the game was well into the second half (about 75 minutes) with the score at 1-0 to Manchester United, who had just gained a direct free kick just outside the Crewe penalty area in a central position. Manchester United's price was 1.20 to back. So I immediately placed £500 on at 1.20.

My thinking was that if Manchester United were to score direct from the free kick, the price would instantly collapse and I would make a nice £100. I also figured that if they were not to score from the free kick, then I could trade out for no loss, or even a small profit due to time running out in the game and the price contracting due to time decay.

Manchester United missed with the free kick and the price went out to 1.22. I decided rather than trade out for a 2 tick loss to let the trade run, hoping to trade out when the price hit 1.19 or 1.20.

What happened next gave me a real jolt – Crewe ran up the other end of the pitch and equalised!

This then left me hoping Manchester United would score a winning goal in the final 10 minutes. The game finished 1-1. Although Manchester United went on to win the game 2-1 in extra time, I was £500 down. Believe me, it is not a great feeling telling your wife you have just blown £500 on a game of football!

This experience turned my trading career and thinking around dramatically. It was after this trade that I started studying the markets in depth, learning all I could about trading philosophy.

Example mistake #2

My second example involves golf.

Early on I believed there could be nothing simpler than laying golfers at fairly long odds not to win tournaments, in the belief they stood no chance. You can go weeks on end without the player you layed ever coming anywhere near the top of the leaderboard.

This particular week I layed Aaron Oberholser in the PGA tournament, for £30 at 15.0 early in the second round. Needless to say the very next day Oberholser was heading the leaderboard way out in front with Co-leader Mike Weir and I had to trade out for a £200 loss.

I suppose the only positive thing I can say about this trade is at least I did manage to halve my potential losses (by closing the position early), as Oberholser went onto to win comfortably on the Sunday evening.

Example mistake #3

My third example is just plain embarrassing, considering my experience, but it just goes to show that, even when you think you are following a plan, bad decisions and ill discipline can still come into play.

Amir Khan was fighting Colombian Breidis Prescott and was priced at 1.14 to win. It was Amir Khan's first pay-per-view fight on Sky TV, with his promoter Frank Warren looking forward to a very long prosperous relationship. Having watched boxing closely over the years I knew that Frank

Warren was extremely shrewd; I could not see him putting Amir Khan at any risk, especially with the new television deal in place.

I figured that I would place £100 on Khan, and, when he won, my winnings would pay for the fee to watch the fight on pay-per-view.

The trade ended up a complete disaster, with Amir Khan being beaten and knocked out inside a minute of the first round.

The lessons

On making a mistake it is vital that you stop and think about what went wrong, and more importantly how you can prevent the same thing from happening again in the future.

Let's look at the three trades above –

1. On the first trade my thinking was probably correct. The free kick was in a very dangerous position and could have easily led to a goal. My mistake here was not cutting out for a loss immediately the free kick did not hit the back of the net. If I had traded out for a 1 or 2 tick loss I would have not lost anything at the end of the game, because Manchester United did not go on to win in normal time.

2. The second trade was completely flawed because by laying Oberholser at odds of 15 (a 6.66% chance of winning), I was backing the rest of the field at 1.07 (a 93.33% chance of winning). A completely ridiculous trade, considering Oberholser was leading during the second round.

3. The third trade was just betting out of boredom – I entered the market because I had nothing better to do, without any pre-planning or preparation. And you should never put on a trade where you are going to lose more than the amount you are trying to win. I have highlighted this because my discipline lapsed and I did not follow my own trading rules that are documented in this book.

The most important thing here is to realise that the big problem for many new traders is that the above three examples could so easily have resulted in winning trades.

I shall just repeat that, because it is so important: the above three examples could, and in all probability should, have ended up being three easy winners.

The mistakes highlighted may not show up for weeks on end, and this can lead to a false sense of security. Then all of a sudden the inevitable happens and the trader gets completely wiped out, ruining weeks of good trading. In reality, the trader had just been lucky all along. This is one of the reasons why it is far better to suffer losses early in your trading career, as lessons quickly learned then eliminate bad trading techniques.

Rule 5: Always learn from your mistakes

On making a mistake do not beat yourself up over it. Stop and think about what went wrong and, more importantly, how you can prevent the same thing from happening again in the future.

8. Keeping a Trading Diary

This is possibly the most important chapter in the book. If you have the discipline to start a trading diary which is reviewed regularly, then this will take your trading to a completely different level.

There is a saying in the Armed Forces –

Do, review, apply

and that is what you are doing here.

You are putting on your trade, reviewing the results of the trade, and, if you are not happy with the results, you can then make changes to your system.

Simply repeat the process of putting on the trade, then reviewing your trades, until you achieve the desired results.

Looking at your profit & loss

Many people who trade on Betfair would argue that to review your trading you just look over the previous three months profit and loss (P&L) results which can be found under 'My Account'. However, although the P&L results are indeed important, it does not show the whole picture of your trading activity.

It misses the following key elements:

1. why the trade was put on, and the thought process behind the trade, and

2. the stop loss and profit objective.

In other words, by only measuring your results by your P&L you will learn little about yourself.

We have already seen in the previous chapters that new traders can get very lucky when they first start trading; simply referring to the P&L to measure progress can hide an awful lot of bad habits and does not show anything about you the trader.

Write it down and follow through on your actions

When you write something down you are demonstrating a real commitment to your goals and that you are going to follow through on your actions.

No matter if you are new to Betfair or have been trading for years, your trading will improve significantly by starting a basic diary. I would also suggest hand writing the diary as opposed to typing the entries, as this focuses the mind more thoroughly on what you are trying to achieve.

The benefits of a good trading diary

1. *A diary helps measure your performance*

    By keeping a diary of your trading you can measure your overall performance in an instant.

2. *Highlights what is working and what is not*

    You can easily pinpoint your strengths and weaknesses, whether this is due to the system you are using, the way you are trading or if the sports you are trading really suit your temperament and personality. After a few weeks of compiling the diary, it will become apparent where you need to improve.

3. *Helps you stick to a plan*

    Many traders find sticking to trading plan rules difficult, but the fact that you are committing your trades to paper will give you the confidence and discipline to follow your system through. Discipline is the glue that holds all trading psychology and systems together. Again, if you discipline yourself to write a diary, your personal discipline should improve in every area.

4. *It highlights all trades both good and bad*

    Many traders seem to suffer from selective memory and tend to forget all the stupid trades they made and just tend to remember all the good trades. A diary shows everything, warts and all.

5. *Highlights areas of specialisation*

    The diary will highlight all those sports that you are good at trading, and not what you think you are good at. You would be surprised by how many traders I come across who dedicate so much time to sports that they are simply no good at trading because they really enjoy the sport and they feel they should also be competent at trading it.

Things to highlight in each diary entry

1. **Time and date of trade.** You may wonder why you need to highlight the time of each trade, but certain people perform better at certain times during the day and week.

2. The **sport and the market traded.**

3. **Why the trade was made.** This section should be filled with comments such as: following a trading plan, or whether you were following the sentiments of experts or websites and newspapers.

4. **How strongly you felt about the trade.** You could use a simple rating system, maybe rating a trade from 1 to 5 to highlight how strong you felt about each trade. This can help in the future as you can rate all your 1 star trades against all of your 5 star trades.

5. **Profit objective.** This is the price that you will be looking to exit the trade.

6. **Stop loss.** Always write down where you have placed your stop loss. This discipline should also ensure that you stick to your stop loss.

7. **Profit/loss.** Finally, you should record how much you have profited or lost from the trade.

Reviewing the diary

Your trading diary should be reviewed at least once a week but ideally once a day.

I spend around half an hour every evening reviewing my trading activity. Initially you should not get too hung up on whether you have profited from your trading.

The most important thing to look for is that, above all else, you made a sensible trading decision that was completely in line with your trading system.

For example, if you have written down a trade that has gone wrong, the fact that you followed your written plan by cutting your losses and getting out as soon as the stop was hit is obviously a very good decision.

Keep two diaries

Personally I keep two diaries –

1. My trading diary which I review every evening.

2. A separate diary in which I look at the next day's sport, and highlight those markets I would be interested in analysing or getting involved with. I also use the second diary to physically plan out my trades, which can be very useful if trading on the outcome of a tennis tournament, or trading on golf.

Take complete responsibility for your results

The path to success involves taking complete responsibility for your actions that ultimately lead to the results – by following the advice in this chapter you will ensure that you begin to do just that.

Rule 6: Keep a trading diary and review it every day

Keep a trading diary that highlights all of your trades and review it every day. I believe that just having the discipline to follow this one rule could improve your trading dramatically.

9. Trading From a Plan

Trading Plans & Systems

Before I explain why you should trade from a plan and use a system, I just want to define the terms so that there is no confusion.

A *trading plan* describes the basic overview, and encompasses all of the disciplines. For example, my current trading plan is to –

- Only trade live televised football, Test match and Twenty20 cricket and NFL.

- Not risk more than £100 per trade.

- Trade the systems and strategies that I have previously tested.

- Keep a trading diary and review my trading weekly.

- Make 20% of my bank per month.

Trading systems on the other hand are the strategies and systems that you will be trading. For example, you may employ one of the tennis systems that are explained at the end of the book. A system is a set of market-specific tactics that have generally proved profitable in the past.

Is the following scenario familiar to you?

You get home from work tired in the evening and have a quick bite to eat before turning on the TV and tuning into Sky Sports. You then decide to log onto the Betfair markets that are related to the event you are about to watch.

If you are the type of person who then begins to work out what you are going to trade, then unfortunately you are in the majority – and are almost certainly destined to fail.

Always do your homework

A good trader will always do his homework on the events he is going to trade. And any trade made will always be part of an overall strategy.

For example, if he is trading a cricket match he will have done his analysis on both of the teams; he will also have looked at any important team news. He will have looked at the state of the pitch and weather conditions and the effects of winning the toss.

Finally he will then look at the odds available and decide on his entry point (already having set up his profit and loss parameters).

In other words he will be fully prepared no matter what happens in the match.

A trading plan should always include:

1. Back and lay points

You should always highlight the back and lay points, as you must always know when and at what point you are going to get in and out of the market.

2. A disciplined money management plan

We shall be dealing with the subject of money management in a later chapter.

3. The plan should suit the trader's style

Importantly the trading plan should suit the trader's style and time frame. It is vital that the trader be comfortable trading in that particular sport, so that he has the confidence to execute the trades when needed.

For example, if you are very analytical you probably would not be comfortable trading a sport like darts, where the price bounces around all over the place within a very small time frame.

Ultimately, though, the biggest advantage of having a trading plan is that you can take full advantage of the market as soon as an obvious opportunity arises.

Compare your trading plan to planning a city break

Trading without a plan can be compared to visiting a large foreign city over a weekend, with no idea of the attractions and places of interest you are going to visit. Wouldn't your trip be far more enjoyable if you knew where you were going, when you were going and what you are going to do once you got there?

And planning for your trip will enable you to get the most out of the *limited time available*. It is the same with Betfair trading.

I always say to those traders who currently have no kind of plan: think of how much better your trading results would be if you knew the following in advance –

- which system you will be using,

- which sports and markets you will be trading,

- how much you are prepared to risk and lose on each trade, and

- what your profit expectation is.

Have a reason for being in the market

Another major advantage to trading with a plan is that sticking strictly to the rules you have set gives you a major reason for actually being in that market. This will then negate the need for those trades that are put on out of boredom.

Also, if you have tested the system you are using, have a positive expectation and your risk is already clearly defined, you are increasing your chances of success dramatically, as you are always remaining both disciplined and focused.

Rule 7: Devise a trading plan

Once you are happy using the Betfair site, and are happy with the markets that you will be trading, take the time to construct a trading plan.

10. Trading Systems

It is almost certain that anyone making a living from Betfair employs a system in their decision-making process. They will all be working to a set of rules which they know produce highly profitable trades.

However, the majority of people trade on Betfair without a system, and these people tend to employ a shotgun approach to their trading. On a typical day they are happy to back a short-priced favourite in a tennis match, and in the next hour or so are then laying the outsider in the evening's televised football match. Then they may end the evening backing a few horses on the American racing.

This type of approach will only lead to inevitable losses.

To be a profitable trader it is essential that you incorporate a trading system into your betting. You also need to follow the rules of the system without question – day in, day out.

Take the decision-making out of your trading

A trading system is simply a set of rules that enable the trader to make a back and lay decision. And the great thing about trading with a system is that you can almost trade without thinking.

A trading system has the following advantages –

- With a system, you don't have to make any decisions as the system does it for you.

- When following the system's rules you know exactly when to enter a trade and, perhaps more importantly, you know when to get out and exit your position.

- It can be a mechanical system where the rules are followed rigidly, or a discretionary system which allows the trader to work freely within a set framework.

- The system can employ both simple and complex rules depending on the results of back-testing previous data.

Ultimately, the point of the system is to enable the trader to make the correct trades that in the past have been shown to be profitable.

Devising the system

Devising a trading system can be extremely arduous and time consuming, as it involves analysing and collecting a great deal of data before you can even begin to see if there any patterns which regularly repeat themselves.

It is a sad fact, however, that many people would just rather get on with trading before considering putting together any type of system.

Ensure the system suits your style

It is imperative that the system suits a trader's trading style, because as with all trading your emotions will still play a large part in the process. For example, various systems –

- may require patience and often no trades will be suggested, which can leave some traders annoyed and frustrated;

- can be very loss averse, whereas other systems can be more risky and the trading far more frequent.

You should find one or more systems that suit your style in the strategies highlighted in the latter section of this book.

Remove the emotion from your trading

Imagine you are trading a Twenty20 match where the runs and wickets are coming thick and fast and the odds are moving up and down very rapidly.

The commentators on the TV are getting excited and your adrenaline is rushing in the anticipation of putting on what you hope will be a successful trade.

By sticking to a mechanical system you are taking away any emotional involvement which, if left unchecked, could play havoc with the balance of your trading account. Trading with a system definitely brings a sense of calm to the situation.

When sticking to your system rules you can calmly place the trade, identifying your stop loss and profitable exit point. There is tremendous excitement as the game draws to a close, but thanks to being disciplined and being completely focused on following your system you are later out of the trade with a profit.

If you did not have a pre-defined system it would have been very easy to get emotionally involved in the game and because of this you could have made completely irrational and costly decisions.

What is the secret to winning on Betfair?

I first became interested in system trading after reading the aforementioned posting on the Betfair forum by 'Troy McClure'.

He was replying, you remember, to someone who asked,

what is the secret to winning on Betfair?

I believe the individual concerned had thought that the best way to profit on Betfair was by placing large sums of money on low priced favourites, and unfortunately had just suffered a large loss.

Troy stated that he thought this individual should not trade for a year but just spend time following the markets. He then suggested he should re-enter trading after analysing and acting on what he had found.

I thought about this for a while, and came to the conclusion that he was completely correct.

I soon found after analysing various markets and studying the resulting charts that, as with the stock market, certain patterns seem to repeat themselves again and again. It is through this study that any trading system is devised.

Spend time analysing the markets

I spend hours analysing data and charts and looking for repeated patterns in various markets, which I then turn into systems similar to those highlighted in the latter part of this book.

Ensure you look at a large sample of data

Always ensure that you analyse as much data as possible. Some initial findings can be encouraging, but as more results and data are analysed you can then discover that they were not consistent.

Sometimes a promising looking system can simply disappear once you have collected enough meaningful data.

For example, this happened to me on analysing one day cricket. On analysing an early sample of charts I realised that a pattern was occurring, such that if you were to lay both teams for £100 at 1.60 it would prove to be very profitable; but as the number of pieces of data increased, this proved not to be the case.

On other occasions the opposite can happen, and what initially did not look encouraging on further investigation can turn out to be very profitable.

So always ensure that when developing a system you analyse as much data as possible.

Just stick with it!

Whether you pay for a system or come up with your own, I would recommend that once it has proved profitable you just stick with it and do not deviate from the system's rules.

Rule 8: Always trade using a system

You must always remember that it is not about the profitability of individual trades, but the consistent results of weeks and months of trading your system that will ultimately prove profitable.

---

11. Learn How the Markets React

We now know that we need a system. And to build a system we need to learn how the markets react.

I often read the forum on the Betfair site to gauge opinion on various sports and trading ideas. One of a number of posts that stuck out for me came again from the successful trader called 'Troy McClure'. I had noticed previously that a number of his posts mentioned the same thing:

> *I just don't understand why people think that backing very low priced favourites is the best way to make money on Betfair.*

These comments usually came after a red hot favourite had narrowly beaten an outsider in a very close-run event. You could tell from the comments left on the forum that there were some very relieved punters. Troy kept on reiterating:

> *Why risk a lot of money to win so little when there are so many low-risk high-return opportunities presenting themselves daily?*

As mentioned in the previous section, he also kept repeating:

> *Study how the markets move for twelve months and then come back and trade what you have learnt.*

To trade any sport you need to get to know how that market moves and behaves under certain conditions. This knowledge alone will improve your chances of becoming profitable. Each sporting market is unique and is affected by certain events occurring. For example –

- In football, when a goal is scored.
- In cricket, when a wicket falls or a boundary is hit.

- In golf, when a shot is dropped or gained.

- In tennis, when a serve is broken.

Ultimately, whichever sport you are trading, you need to get to know how the market reacts to these events.

Possibly more importantly, when you start to specialise in one or two sports you will get to learn the behaviour of the markets, and you will also see that certain patterns repeat themselves time and time again. This is what I base the majority of my trading on.

Aim to trade on price alone

After extensively studying the tennis markets and how they react, I am now trading on price alone. In many circumstances I cannot even pronounce the names of the two players involved in the match. I do look at a simple live scoreboard, but that is only to tell me if we are in the early or late stages of a match.

Whilst we are on the subject of trading sport, when watching it on live TV I find that I trade better when just watching the price movement and a simple scorecard. For myself I generally tend to do this with tennis and cricket. Although I do tend to have the cricket on in the background, the sound is always muted.

The only sports I trade whilst watching are football and golf. In the case of golf, I am very aware that the live coverage can be some minutes behind, but essentially I am trading by looking at the scoreboard on the PGA website and watching the price on Betfair.

Turn off the TV and you turn off your emotions

I believe that if you are watching the event whilst trading, there could be a tendency to become emotionally involved with the match and the trade you are placing.

These days sport is all razzmatazz and this is reflected in the coverage, with over-excited commentators building up every event. Unfortunately, in trading you have to keep all emotions in check, and I believe that once you have confidence in your trading system the actual act of watching the event live is secondary.

I would also never get involved in trading any event you have a personal interest in. For example, never back your favourite football, rugby or cricket team – you will be too involved emotionally in the trade and your well thought out plans could very easily fly out the window.

My advice is keep your emotions in check, and at the very least mute your TV when watching the sport.

Rule 9: Learn how the markets react

Spend a year watching how the markets behave and then build a plan around your findings.

12. Back-testing

After doing some research, hopefully you will have devised a trading system that you believe will work. You are now left with a number of options. You can either –

1. go straight into trading the system with real money, or

2. spend some time paper trading the system.

However, the best way of forming a true opinion of whether the system will be profitable or not is by back-testing to see how the system performed in the past.

Will the system be profitable in the future?

The great thing about back-testing is the fact that if the plan does not show a profit during the back-testing process, then it is probably right to assume that it will not show a profit going forward in the future!

When it comes to back-testing, the advantage of trading the Betfair markets as opposed to the more traditional financial markets is that there are so many more examples where the framework and parameters are similar.

Add confidence to your plan with sheer numbers

When analysing the financial markets, the experts usually recommend that you look at at least 30 to 40 sets of data in order to devise and back-test your system. However, on Betfair there are so many markets you can back-test hundreds of sets of data.

For example, in the tennis data highlighted at the end of this book, I have analysed over 700 sets of data. And with the example of the strategy used, I have highlighted over 380 matches that had exactly the same parameters –

- They were all best of 3 set matches.

- They were all favourites with a starting price between 1.21 – 1.50.

This amount of data adds real confidence to your back-testing and trading plan.

Ensure you have at least 100 sets of data

On the sporting markets I believe you need to have at least 100 sets of data, and preferably 300 before you can begin to make a valid argument for a system.

As an example, last year I analysed data on one day cricket matches and it soon became apparent after around 50 matches' worth of analysis that a distinct trend was beginning to form. It was proving profitable to lay both teams at 1.60. Indeed at one stage I was looking at a profit of over £350 to £1 a tick stakes. However, once the number of recorded games raised to over 150 the validity of the system did not hold, and indeed after 157 games I was looking at a loss of just over £300.

Optimising the data

With back-testing you can –

1. optimise your plan to increase your profits, or

2. set the win to loss ratio.

An example of this is also shown in the tennis strategy at the end of this book.

However, this does come with a word of warning. By optimising the data, you can make the mistake of making the plan far too complicated to follow and the results can be false.

Test your system on future events

Once you have devised a system, you should *always* test it on future events before trading with real cash, as the system you are thinking of using (although profitable) could produce a very high number of consecutive losers before producing the expected profit.

This can have a major impact on your confidence and faith in the system, and you should allow for all possible eventualities as the drawdown can happen quickly. You should be fully prepared for any losing run.

This is why, when you make small adjustments to any system, it is imperative to test it on future events to ensure that the plan is still workable.

How to back-test a system

OK, you have analysed the markets and believe you may potentially have a workable system.

For example, you have noticed that in a basketball game a favourite (priced between 1.40 and 1.60) that takes a decisive early lead in the first quarter of a match tends to trade below 1.25. You have also noticed that with three quarters of the match remaining, this gives the opposition ample time to get back into the game. On your initial observations you see that this is indeed the case and the price of the favourite often rises by 30 to 50 ticks (to between 1.40 – 1.75) when the opposition start getting back into the match.

The question is: how do you go about proving this?

The best way of back-testing a system is to get hold of some previous charts and graphs. These are available at Betfair (data.betfair.com) or from Fracsoft (www.fracsoft.com).

If you decide to use Fracsoft and wish to analyse some basketball matches, you are looking at spending 0.11p per match or £11 to analyse 100 matches.

This is cash well spent, as it can save you a lot of time and money in seeing if your system is profitable.

Once you have hold of the data it is then just a case of creating a chart and analysing the price movement. On Fracsoft, the software does this for you and actually displays the odds' movement in real time.

By then analysing a reasonable number of games you can see if your system is indeed profitable. If you do find that your system is profitable, I suggest that you then watch the price movement of current in-play matches to make sure that your system does absolutely work.

The next stage, once you are happy that your system is profitable, is to then start trading the system with real money, confident that you should be showing a positive return.

Rule 10: Spend time back-testing your system

The best way of forming a true opinion of whether a trading system will be profitable or not, is by back-testing to see how the system would have performed in the past. Ensure that you test at least 100, and preferably 300, pieces of data.

13. Make Sure Your Strategy Has Been Historically Profitable

Although this may sound blindingly obvious, you must always ensure that the system you are trading has a solid history of profitability.

A good example of organisations that have systems that show profitability over time are:

- casinos,

- gaming machine halls, and

- bookmakers.

All three of these organisations may suffer the odd loss now again, but in the end the odds are well and truly stacked on their side.

Indeed, so sure are they of their profitability that casinos very often give away free nights in their most expensive suites to their big money winners; they know that they will get their money back. The system they are working will always show a positive return – and so must yours.

Winners outperforming losers

The first rule should be to never get bogged down with win/loss ratios. So long as your system is financially profitable and your winning trades outperform your losing trades that is all you should be worried about.

For example, if your system shows a 40% win to 60% loss ratio, and your average win is £70 and your average loss is £25, then the overall expectancy of this system out of ten trades would be –

```
Winners 4 x £70 = £280; losers 6 x £25 = £150
```

Leaving a profit over the 10 trades of £130. So in this example your average profit per trade would be £13.

This is then the task of your back-testing: to find the system that is going to bring in the largest profit per trade.

The following two examples refer to the tennis strategy presented in the appendix.

Example 1

The strategy that highlighted greening up at 1.50 showed the following (of 416 matches):

- 204 winners
- 101 losers
- 111 no bets

This left a profit of £4480 (£10.76 profit per trade including the no bets).

Example 2

On greening up at 2.0, the results show the following (of 416 matches):

- 146 winners
- 159 losers
- 111 no bets

This left a profit of £6095 (£14.65 profit per trade including the no bets).

As you can see, both sets of data produced a healthy profit; however, the greening up at 2.0 – although showing 58 more losers – produced £1615 more in profit.

This is where you learn what type of trader you are.

If you are less risk averse, I would recommend the first strategy. If you can take more losses, then the second strategy is better.

Sports that produce profitable strategies

I believe tennis, cricket, darts, snooker and basketball lend themselves best to back-testing (and thus producing profitable strategies).

Football

At this point (although I will be covering this in more depth later) I would like to mention football.

This is definitely not a sport where I would look to devise a general strategy that can be used on any and all matches. The game has been analysed so much that there is virtually no edge to be had.

Indeed, I believe it would be very difficult to find a consistently profitable strategy that could be employed on each and every game.

Trade each game individually

However, that does not mean that you cannot trade individual games successfully; it just means that you have to do some thorough homework.

For example, in the 2009 season Aston Villa were away to Stoke; and in Aston Villa's previous matches they tended to score plenty of goals in the second half. I advised about the game in question on my blog, and recommended laying under 2.5, and 1.5 if the game was scoreless after 25 minutes or so. And so my advice proved sound, with Stoke running out 3-2 winners, with late goals in the second half.

So my advice for trading football would be to do your homework every time, and stick to individual trades.

Rule 11: Ensure your strategy has historic profitability

Always ensure that your system has a solid history of profitability, and that on looking back in the past your winning trades have outperformed your losing trades.

14. Randomness and High Probability Trades

In our daily lives we generally observe that things happen in a certain way, and we also perceive a sense of predictability to these events.

For example, although we have house insurance which protects us should we be unfortunate enough to suffer, say, a fire, we never actually think that it is us that will have the fire. We say that it will never happen to us.

It will never happen to me

But the fact remains that it does happen to some people, and it happens every day. As time goes by and the fire does not happen, we feel more certain that it will never happen to us. Then if the fire does occur, we naturally think of it as a complete fluke.

In fact, most people actually create the fire that burns their home and property.

People who have a drink and smoke in their house don't really believe that the problem was entirely their own if a fire results. Yet it was their poor judgement that increased the odds of this so-called random event happening. Because they stub out their cigarettes 99% of the time without any incident occurring, they fail to grasp that during the 1% of the time when they are drunk and smoking, the 99% success rate is now completely null and void and the rules of the game are completely different.

Insurance companies understand that these 'random' events happen virtually everyday. So they spread the risk that this will happen to as many people as it will. Indeed, they will sell as many policies to as many people to whom the event will almost certainly never happen (i.e. non-smokers) as they can.

We should therefore approach our trading like an insurance company approaches fire hazards – by finding the high probability trades (as the insurance company seeks out the non-smoker).

Randomness and sport

One thing that needs to remembered – and many people fail to grasp this – is: once you put your money in the market anything can happen. If we knew what was going to happen, we could make a living with a crystal ball at the end of the pier!

This is the beauty and attraction of sport – it is, at times, completely unpredictable.

Counter randomness and find high probability trades

The best way of countering randomness in the market is to distinguish between the high and low probability trades, and to patiently wait for the low risk, high opportunity trades.

This is where there is a distinct difference between gambling and trading.

A gambler places his money in the market without any sort of reason or plan in the hope that that the odds will move in the right direction. A trader follows a strict trading plan with a good money management plan, and only makes selective trades that have a high probability of working and ultimately being profitable.

A high probability trade has a proven historical record of working, and generally the financial risk is low compared to the amount that can be made. When executing this trade you should be able to explain to someone, in plain English, the logic of what you are doing, the risk involved, and the level of profit you are aiming to achieve.

Be patient and wait for the opportunity

When seeking high profitability trades, it is essential to be patient and wait for the opportunities to present themselves. This is where specialisation and a particular knowledge of a sport become invaluable.

If you don't see a good trade, then you simply do not trade. If you are keeping an up-to-date diary (as explained in a previous chapter) these high probability trades should soon jump out at you and become very apparent.

One of the advantages of restricting yourself to this type of trading opportunity is that you can alter and increase your position size, which then allows you to take full advantage of the situation.

An example of a high probability trade

As previously mentioned, I like to specialise in the pre-match under 2.5 goal markets. A very good opportunity presented itself in a Community Shield match between Manchester United and Portsmouth.

After doing all my research the day before the game, I believed the price on the under 2.5 goal market should have been somewhere between 1.68 and 1.84.

I was also encouraged by the fact that Manchester United were struggling to find a fully fit strike force for the match. When I went to log on to Betfair, the under 2.5 goal price was around 1.92/1.94.

I realised that this was a fantastic opportunity to cash in, and I immediately had £750 matched at 1.93. I went on to green up just before kick off at 1.72, which left me with a healthy profit of £91.56 (or 12.2% return) before the game had started.

Incidentally, the game went on to finish 0-0, but the point is not the result but the fact that the match was incorrectly priced from the outset.

This was a great example of a high probability trade –

1. the **risk** was minimal,

2. the **profit margin** was good, and

3. there was also a reason for me to be **in the market**.

I knew through experience that the trade was only ever going to go one way.

> *Note:* It would be very wrong to presume that trades like the one highlighted happen on a very regular basis. But if you are prepared to do the relevant homework, they do occur often enough to ensure that you can make yourself a decent regular profit.

Rule 12: Only trade high probability trades

A high probability trade has a proven historical record of working and generally the financial risk is low compared to the amount that can be made. When executing this trade, you should be able to explain to someone in plain English the logic of what you are doing, the risk involved, and the level of profit you are aiming to achieve.

15. Mistakes and Warning Signs

Overtrading

I was going to write a section featuring examples of traders who I have met, and the common mistakes they are making.

But I think you should know by now, that:

- you are always expected to cut your losses quickly, and

- you should always stake yourself correctly in proportion to your available bank.

However, there is one very bad habit that really does need to be highlighted, and that is overtrading.

A case study

I know of one trader, who, when it comes to analysing and reading a game of cricket, is quite frankly a genius. He plots out the future possible scenarios like a chess master ponders over his next few moves.

He knows exactly the right time in a match, when the odds are very much in his favour, to lay a side. He can do this for both Test matches, and one day games. He also knows where to place his profitable exit and stop loss points.

However, he does suffer from one problem; overtrading.

Through overtrading he –

- does not follow his own rules and plans,

- is increasing the number of mistakes he is making in the market, and

- is turning a winning position into a losing position far too regularly.

If he just stuck to his own plans, he would be an extremely successful trader.

It got to the stage where he just would not learn from his own mistakes and I suggested that he quit trading completely; he was simply wasting his time and money.

An example of overtrading

During a match, his plan was to lay a team at 1.25 and then back them at 1.50. He would then set a stop loss at around 1.15.

His logic made complete sense.

However, once he entered the market, he would not let the trade run to its logical conclusion.

Many times the price would go down to 1.20, and he would ignore his stop loss, and take a loss far too quickly.

He would then re-enter the market a few minutes later, when the price went back up to 1.25.

Unfortunately, the markets this guy liked trading were generally flat, choppy markets and did not move unless something decisive happened. Consequently he would cut his losses frequently, and these small losses would then start building up to a substantial amount of money.

When the market did eventually move his way, he was now so scared of taking another loss that he would then cut out of the market far too quickly, exiting at the 1.35 level.

This trader forgot that exiting winners early is just as bad as not stopping losses at the right point.

This situation then put him in a panic, and, as the small losses began to build up, he then began taking bigger risks in order to recoup these losses.

Completely ignoring his plan

At this stage, one of the teams would be priced at around 1.35 to go on and win the match.

Now he would completely ignore his previously thought-out plan, and put on a substantial amount of money backing the team at 1.35, hoping to wipe out his previous losing trades.

Obviously in sport nothing is that straightforward, and often as not the price of the team he had backed would go out to around 2.0, and through various ill-judged trades he would then end up showing a large loss whatever the result.

It really is unbelievable the number of times he went on to completely lose his whole bank.

Summary

As previously stated, you really need discipline and patience to follow many of these strategies, and this can prove very difficult for many traders – many feel that they should always be in the market doing something.

You must constantly remember to stick to your plan, and remember that it is all right to have losing days. This is part and parcel of trading. You must learn to take the loss, and move straight on to the next pre-planned trade that fits into your system, rather than overtrading.

Gambling Addiction

I worked in a bookmakers around 25 years ago, and have seen at first hand the devastation an addiction to gambling can cause. I personally view trading on Betfair as a hobby and a challenge, and when I place my money in the market I know that I can afford to lose the money that I am trading and that I am placing my money on a calculated risk.

If my trades are successful I enjoy the rewards; but if not, I put it down to experience, review my trading plan and carry on.

Because I am not trading with money that I cannot afford to lose, my mindset is always the same.

A case study

As an example, I was mentoring a trader who was doing really well. Although he was not following a system mechanically, his trades were always well thought out.

Initially, I believed he was well capitalised, and that his bank was growing in line with his ability and confidence. I believed he had the makings of being a very successful, highly profitable trader – until one crazy Saturday.

On this particular day he was trading on snooker. The trade went against him and he had failed to utilise his stop loss. He then changed direction completely, and backed the other player. However, once again, the trade went against him, and he had undone all the good work from the previous few weeks.

He had a starting bank of £1000. The bank had grown to just under £2000, and after the snooker it fell to just under £700. I spoke to him on the phone and said that he was not to worry. We would pick it up again in the next week, and start again with the basics. At this time, I believed he had just got carried away and had basically suffered from a lapse of discipline and concentration.

From bad to worse

When I spoke to him again on the Tuesday of the following week, he informed me that he had nothing left in his betting bank.

On the Monday he had layed a horse at 1.69 for £1000, the horse went on to win, and it had cleaned his account out. From what I can understand, there were plenty of opportunities to trade out for a profit during the race, but he just sat there helpless as the horse went on to win.

He then went on to explain that the money he was using came from an overdraft, and that prior to opening an account on Betfair he had lost large sums of money in previous years just backing straight selections with the bookmakers. He thought it might somehow be different trading on the Betfair markets. I suggested to this individual that he was best closing his account, and seeking professional help for his gambling problem.

The above is a very sad story, but unfortunately it is not an isolated one. There are hundreds of people who should not be going anywhere near the betting exchanges.

Below is a list of behaviours that can signal that there may be problems

1. **The inability to stop trading**

    These people trade on anything and everything. They are unable to control the time or money they spend on the markets, and invariably play until there is literally nothing left in their account.

2. **Chasing losses**

    These traders never like ending the day with a loss, and they end up taking bigger and bigger risks in order to win back what they have previously lost. Very often this works, but in the end their banks are normally wiped out.

3. **Borrowing money to trade**

    This creates real problems. Money that should be allocated to household expenditure is spent trading the markets. Once lost, they may start taking out loans or second mortgages to carry on funding their habit.

4. **Lying to conceal losses**

    This is an ever downward spiral, as the trader after suffering heavy losses then begins lying to spouse, family and friends in order to conceal the extent of his debt.

5. **A preoccupation with trading**

    These people tend to think about nothing else but trading. They then start to appear preoccupied and distant and this can then start affecting their health.

If you, or anyone you know, shows any symptoms of the above, then I would definitely recommend that they stop trading and seek professional help.

PART THREE

Money Management and Risk

16. Protecting Your Bank

Possibly the most important aspect of money management is protecting what you already have (i.e. your trading bank). When trading, you should try to forget about the winning and concentrate on not losing – this should be your first priority.

To be successful you need to stay in the game, and the only way to achieve this is by keeping your losses small. It is not how much you win that counts, but how little you lose that ultimately shows where you stand in the trading game.

Treat your money with the respect it deserves

In the previous section I spoke about only trading with money you can afford to lose. Although you may actually be able to afford to lose this money, you should *never* go into the market with the mindset that you can happily do so.

You have worked hard for this money, and you need to treat your trading bank with the respect it deserves.

In today's online and credit-driven world it is very easy to spend money we do not really have. It is also very easy to open an account with Betfair and deposit money.

Indeed, it is quite possible today to go through daily life with barely the need to see actual money. I believe we never truly appreciate the real value of money as all we ever see from our bank account statements and our credit card bills is abstract figures. We forget the fact that for most of us to acquire this money we have had to give up our most precious commodity, that of time.

I always equate the money won and lost in my account to the time it would take to work to earn the money. This really brings home the reality of the situation, and therefore I am always more than keen on preserving my hard-earned capital.

The reality of money

To get you to think on the same wavelength, I would suggest the following tips –

1. **For one week, purchase everything with cash only.**

    You will be amazed how your attitude to money changes immediately by physically handing over real cash instead of the usual debit/credit cards. Indeed, if you try this for a month, it could have some far-reaching effects and transform your attitude to money for the rest of your life.

2. **Keep a £5 and £20 note by your computer whilst trading.**

    Although this may sound strange, if you ever doubt whether or not you should get out of a trade that is going in the wrong direction, and you are hesitant to use your stop loss, look at the £5 and £20 note and ask yourself, "If I was to lose one of these notes which would it be? Would I rather lose the £5 or the £20?" This focuses the mind on the reality of the situation.

Of course this also has a positive effect on your winning trades, because you then appreciate the amount you have won more than when it was just a figure displayed on a computer screen.

Winning starts with a solid defence

In recent years I have played snooker with people of varying abilities, but none of them outstanding. In these games you certainly learn the art of defence. Nearly all of the games were won by the individual or couple who made the least mistakes – not by how many balls we potted.

Success in managing risk starts with a good solid defence. Before entering any trade you should always asses the risk first, and know beforehand when you are going to get out. When you commit to following this rule before doing anything, then everything else should start falling into place.

Following this rule means that you are in complete control of the situation, no matter what the outcome.

Rule 13: Protect your bank

To preserve your bank, before entering any trade you should always asses the risk first and know beforehand when you are going to get out of the trade.

---

17. A Money Management Plan

There is no question about it; money management is a vital ingredient in ensuring your success in the sporting markets. A good money management system moves you away from making ill-conceived, emotional decisions and takes you towards a well-considered plan in order to protect you from making rash judgements.

Money and the mind

When money is concerned, it is a fact that most of us at times make some ridiculous decisions.

For example, say you and a friend have tossed a coin and the winner receives £5 from the other player. If you win £5, you are less likely to offer double or quits; but should you lose the £5, you are more than likely to want to take a greater risk, in order just to get your money back.

When looking at the example above, it is very easy to see how the mind works when faced with a loss. On the Betfair markets, you can very easily go for months steadily building up profits; and then all it takes is one moment of indiscipline that, without correct risk management, can wipe out all of that money accumulated over the previous weeks. You are then left with nothing.

Without a good, robust money management plan, you will almost certainly at some stage lose all of your money.

My personal money management plan is simple yet effective; there are four easy rules to follow.

1. **Identify the markets you are happy trading.**

   Ensure you understand what makes the markets move and that you have a system to play these markets.

2. **Pre-define your entry and exit position.**

   Through your system, decide your entry and exit positions (both stop loss and profit target). Always ensure that you can explain logically the exact reason as to why you are putting your money on at this point in the market. Through back-testing your system you should have identified the best place to put your stop loss.

3. **Calculate your position size using the 1%-2% rule.**

   Always ensure that you are never risking more than 2% of your bank on any single trade.

4. **Execute the trade.**

   When the moment arrives (and only then) execute the trade in line with your plan.

How much should be risked on each trade

The idea of a money management system is to keep you in the game when you inevitably experience a losing run. When trading on Betfair, I look to risk 1%-2% of my total bank. As I generally work with a bank of £5000, that means I am risking £50 a trade.

The following tables highlight the effect on your trading account should you suffer 20 losses in a row.

In the first table we are assuming that you have a bank of £1000, and you are prepared to risk 1% of your bank on each trade.

So on your first trade you have risked £10 (1% of £1000), and your trade has been unsuccessful.

This then leaves you with a bank of £990.

So on your next trade you are risking £9.90 (which is 1% of 990), and so the table goes on; until after 20 losing trades your bank is now down to £817.91.

Should you have been trading 2% of your bank, then this figure is reduced to £667.61.

Table 3.1: Trading with 1% of bank

Trade	Amount lost	Account balance
		£1000.00
1	£10.00	£990.00
2	£9.90	£980.10
3	£9.80	£970.30
4	£9.70	£960.60
5	£9.61	£950.99
6	£9.51	£941.48
7	£9.41	£932.07
8	£9.32	£922.74
9	£9.23	£913.52
10	£9.14	£904.38
11	£9.04	£895.34
12	£8.95	£886.38
13	£8.86	£877.52
14	£8.78	£868.75
15	£8.69	£860.06
16	£8.60	£851.46
17	£8.51	£842.94
18	£8.43	£834.51
19	£8.35	£826.17
20	£8.26	£817.91

Table 3.2: Trading with 1.5% of bank

Trade	Amount lost	Account balance
		£1000.00
1	£15.00	£985.00
2	£14.78	£970.23
3	£14.55	£955.67
4	£14.34	£941.34
5	£14.12	£927.22
6	£13.91	£913.31
7	£13.70	£899.61
8	£13.49	£886.11
9	£13.29	£872.82
10	£13.09	£859.73
11	£12.90	£846.83
12	£12.70	£834.13
13	£12.51	£821.62
14	£12.32	£809.30
15	£12.14	£797.16
16	£11.96	£785.20
17	£11.78	£773.42
18	£11.60	£761.82
19	£11.43	£750.39
20	£11.26	£739.14

Table 3.3: Trading with 2% of bank

Trade	Amount lost	Account balance
		£1000.00
1	£20.00	£980.00
2	£19.60	£960.40
3	£19.21	£941.19
4	£18.82	£922.37
5	£18.45	£903.92
6	£18.08	£885.84
7	£17.72	£868.13
8	£17.36	£850.76
9	£17.02	£833.75
10	£16.67	£817.07
11	£16.34	£800.73
12	£16.01	£784.72
13	£15.69	£769.02
14	£15.38	£753.64
15	£15.07	£738.57
16	£14.77	£723.80
17	£14.48	£709.32
18	£14.19	£695.14
19	£13.90	£681.23
20	£13.62	£667.61

As you can see from the preceding tables, using a strict 1% risk of your bank on each trade, you would have to suffer a run of incredibly bad luck in order for your trading account to be completely wiped out.

After deciding what percentage of your bank you are going to risk on each trade, you then have to calculate your position size for each trade.

How to calculate position size

We will assume that you are working with a bank of £1000 and you are looking to make the following trades.

Example 1

- You are laying a selection at 1.50 with a stop loss of 1.25. You are risking 1% of your £1000 bank, which is £10.

- Your stop loss is 25 ticks away (1.50 - 1.25 = .25) so you divide the £10 by 25 which leaves you with £0.40p a tick.

So you would lay this selection for £40.

Example 2

- Again, you are laying a selection at 1.50 but this time the stop loss is placed at 1.40. You are risking 1% of your £1000 bank which is £10.

- Your stop loss is 10 ticks away (1.50 - 1.40 = .10) so you divide the £10 by 10 which leaves you with £1.00 a tick.

So you would lay this selection for £100.

As you can see by the above examples, the stop loss has made a great difference to the amount you are trading per tick (in the above case it is 60p).

Never move your predetermined stop loss in order to trade more per tick. Your stop loss is there for a purpose – it is the point where you will have decided that this trade is not working and you need to minimise your risk and exit the trade now.

Always know your profit objective

You can never be a completely successful trader without having a predefined plan for exiting your winning trades at the correct time.

Knowing your winning objective is vital, because at some stage you are going to have to make the decision to close the trade. The best time to do this is to decide your exit and entry points *before* entering the market.

Having a predefined exit point helps you to develop discipline in your trading system.

Focus on stop loss and exit

As you will have no doubt experienced, the markets are in a constant state of change and at times can seem chaotic. By having an exit point, it helps you focus on the two points that are really important –

1. the stop loss, and

2. the exiting of the winning trade.

With the constant price movement it is very easy to get distracted and take your eye off your system. But by not keeping to your entry and exit points there is a dangerous tendency to overtrade. (I will be dealing with overtrading in a later section.)

Risk/reward ratios

A risk/reward ratio is used by many traders to compare the expected returns of a trade to the size of risk undertaken to capture these returns.

The ratio is calculated by dividing the amount of profit the trader expects to have made when the position is closed by the amount he stands to lose if the position goes wrong.

For example, the price of the draw in the Test match has gone down to 1.30. You have just placed a £300 lay bet on the draw at 1.30 and you have placed a stop-loss at 1.20 to ensure that your losses will not exceed £30. You are expecting a couple of wickets to fall in the next hour or so, and anticipating that the draw price will move out to 1.65. Once the price hits 1.65, you will exit the trade and green up for a profit.

In this scenario your profit would be £105 (the difference between laying £300 at 1.30 and backing £300 at 1.65) / 1.65.

This then leads to a profit of £63.63 from your initial risk of £30.

As you stand to make double the amount that you have risked, you would be said to have a 2:1 risk/reward ratio on this particular trade.

How you define your exit point using ratios

Defining your risk/reward ratios helps you to set your exit point. Without this, in my experience, there is a tendency for the inexperienced trader to not hold on to winning trades, closing them far earlier than is necessary. Ultimately, this means you will never be able to overcome your losses.

I will give you three examples using the tennis stats for setting risk/reward ratios, and to illustrate the dangers of not setting exit points and working to these ratios.

We will look at the strategy that looks to back a player at 2.0 after laying £100 at 1.25 and a further £200 at 1.13.

On each of these trades there is a possible loss of £51.

We will look at the following three scenarios:

1. *Leaving the bet.*
   If we simply leave the bet, then the potential profit is £300 – which gives a risk/reward ratio of just under 6/1 (£300/£51).

2. *Backing the selection at 2.0 and then letting the trade run.*
   If we back the selection at 2.0 and let the trade run the potential profit is £249, which gives a risk/reward ratio of just under 5/1 (£249/£51).

3. *Greening up at 2.0 and equally distributing the profits.*
   If we green up at 2.0 and then equally distribute the profits, the potential profit is £124.50 which gives a risk/reward ratio of 2.5/1 (£124.50/£51).

On the above we have effectively layed £300 at 1.17 (£100 at 1.25 then £200 at 1.13). There is no stop loss so we are risking £51 and the exit point is 2.0. So we have already predefined our exit and entry points.

We have analysed the system and it looks profitable – all we now need to do is execute the trade.

Personally I think risk/reward ratios are useful if you are developing a system similar to the tennis strategies described above (and in more detail later in the book).

However, as a general rule of thumb, I never look to lose more on a trade than I am trying to win. If you keep this in mind you should not go too far wrong.

Rule 14: Risk only 1–2% of your bank on any one trade

Always ensure you follow the four rules of the money management plan and never risk more than 2% of your bank on any one trade.

PART FOUR

Trading Psychology

18. Learning to Accept Losses

Without doubt this is the hardest discipline to learn if you are going to trade the Betfair markets with any success.

 You have to accept the fact that losing is always going to be a part of trading.

You will never be perfect

If you are a perfectionist or you take your losses personally, then I am afraid this is certainly not the game for you. Throughout our lives we are conditioned not to make mistakes, and in our day-to-day work we are trained to avoid failure at any cost. A loss or a mistake is seen as totally unacceptable.

This does not work in trading, as the very essence of trading involves risk-taking, where losses are inevitable. It is how we accept and handle them that is important.

As a beginner you should deal with your losses in the following ways –

1. Not blame anything for your losses.

2. Accept them as the cost of doing business and educating yourself.

3. Never let a loss influence your future trades.

4. Stick to your trading system and plan.

Remember that the important issue here is not so much how much money you make on a particular trade, but how little you lose on the losses – *this* is really the key to profitable trading.

Accept you will lose

Let's look at the following scenario.

You have been working on a trading system for the Twenty20 cricket and you have back-tested over 100 matches. You have come to the following conclusions: you realise with your system you only need to have 4 winners out of 10 matches to make a reasonably good profit. It is at this time you believe that the system will work for you.

However – and this needs to be emphasised very strongly – before putting money on the trade, you have to *accept fully* that you can lose the amount of money you are risking on this trade.

Providing the amount of money you are risking is measured and part of your plan (which we will cover more of later), then through continued practice this should eventually become achievable.

If you can learn this discipline it will put you in a position where you will be able to attack your trading, taking advantage of every available opportunity that presents itself.

Your attitude to risk is all in the mind

Your mindset and how you perceive your risk-taking is everything.

If you are happy in your mind to take the risk, you will be free to follow your system confidently, and your success should follow as you have probability on your side.

On the other hand, if you are not happy taking the risk, the system will eventually go out of the window. You will start panicking after a few losses, putting on bigger and riskier trades.

As with any new skill, this needs to be practised thoroughly over a period of time. This is an extremely challenging discipline to master, so begin slowly and increase your stakes only when you are completely happy to accept your losses.

This is definitely one of the hardest rules to follow but once mastered you are well on the way to success.

Rule 15: Accept fully that you may lose the amount risked on each trade

You are not going to win on every trade and you have to accept that some of your trades are going to be losers. Accept this and discipline yourself to stick with your planned system.

19. Be a Contrarian

Imagine you are watching golf on a Sunday evening, and a player you fancy to win the competition has just birdied the 9th hole to go 4 shots clear in the final round of this televised event. You watch as his price drops like a stone from around 1.80 to 1.55, and you decide to follow the crowd and the money in backing this particular golfer at the current available price of 1.50. He then tees off on the 10th, only to see his ball take a massive hook and land out of bounds. After taking a double bogey, his price has now risen to 2.12 and you are left with the possibility of showing a hefty loss.

The above scenario will be familiar to many. You perceive something as a sure thing and back it heavily at low odds, expecting your selection to win comfortably.

However, this is very rarely the case and, as with the above example, you are often holding a trade for an uncomfortable hour or so, hoping your sure-fire selection will go on to win.

Televised sport was made to be unpredictable

Today, live televised sporting events are big business. They attract huge audiences and massive sponsorship deals. The reason these events attract such attention is that they are exciting and on many occasions go right down to the wire, with the underdogs often coming back from what seemed impossible odds.

In these scenarios we should look to –

1. devise strategies and systems to profit, and
2. get into the mindset where we are opposing what we perceive will happen.

Incredible comebacks

There are examples of incredible comebacks in all sports; you would be amazed how often a 1.01 priced favourite fails to go on and win. Take a look at some of the following examples.

- Football – everyone can remember Liverpool's famous comeback to win the Champions League Final after being 0-3 down at half-time to AC Milan.

- Tennis – there is not a week that goes by where a player does not come back from match point down to eventually win.

- Cricket – in the Twenty20 or one day matches, all it takes is an incredible over of batting or bowling to completely turn the match from what seemed like an unwinnable position.

- Golf – there are so many hazards on the course, as well as the competitiveness of the rest of the field, that can prevent a player from winning from what initially would seem a very comfortable position.

The idea of contrary thinking is not so much that you don't think a player who is four shots ahead with six holes to play is not going to win the competition. It is getting into the mindset where when you place a trade you have little to lose but a lot to gain.

 It is also the knowing when to go against the crowd. You know that in the past winning from this position has never been plain sailing and the odds are going to swing dramatically before the final putt is sunk.

Examples of contrary thinking

As an example of how we may think contrary to the general consensus of opinion, I present below six charts from the NBA, Indian Premier League cricket and womens tennis Open in Warsaw.

These six charts were just a sample of the opportunities available everyday on Betfair; they all took place between Monday 18th - Thursday 21st May 2009.

This sample of data, although offering no system or strategy, is just to highlight the kind of scenarios we would be looking to exploit.

The charts represent the prices available on Betfair and we can see that by taking a low-risk, disciplined approach, profits can be regularly made. After each chart I shall give a brief indication of where profits could have been made.

Aleksandra Wozniak v Julia Goerges (6–7, 6–3) WTA Warsaw Open Monday 18th May 2009

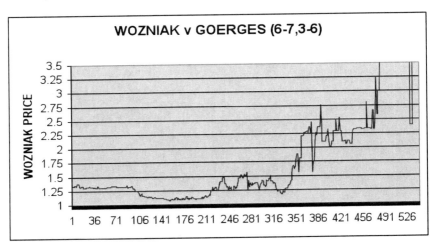

The chart represents the Betfair price of Aleksandra Wozniak.

Start of match odds Aleksandra Wozniak: 1.32.

This should not take much thought. At 1.07 during the first set after breaking serve, Wozniak would have to be layed. If, for example, you layed her for £200 to lose £14, and looked to green out at 50 ticks later 1.57, you could have greened out for £63 profit.

Although it may sound as though I am repeating myself, these are the type of low-risk trades you should be looking to execute. Not much to lose but everything to gain.

Kolkata v Chennai, Indian Premier League Monday 18th May 2009

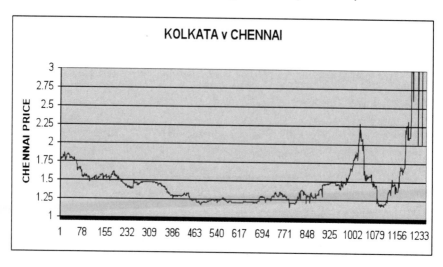

The chart represents the Betfair price of Chennai.

Start of match odds Chennai 1.78.

After averaging 9.4 an over and scoring 188, Chennai were strong favourites, trading at 1.15 against an out of form Kolkata.

I think it needs to be highlighted again that there is such an overreaction in these prices, and Chennai are a good lay trade. And so it proved, as Brendon McCullum and Bradley Hodge set about the Chennai attack.

You have to think that even if Kolkata started their innings poorly you could still get out at around 1.10.

 This example clearly shows that by keeping a cool head, going against the crowd and minimising your risks, excellent profits can be made.

Edina Gallovits v Jill Craybas (6-3, 5-7, 3-6) WTA Warsaw Open Tuesday 19th May 2009

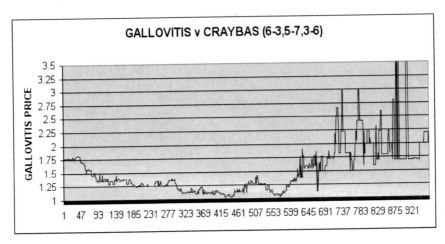

The chart represents the Betfair price of Edina Gallovits.

Start of match odds Edina Gallovits 1.75.

After winning the first set and breaking serve in the second set Gallovits was trading as low as 1.03. It only takes a quick break of serve and the price can shoot up dramatically.

Again, a trade where there is little to lose and everything to gain.

Orlando v Cleveland 107–106 NBA Conference Finals Wednesday 20th May 2009

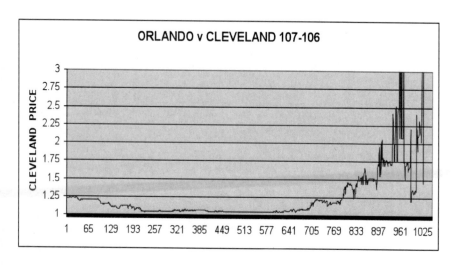

The chart represents the Betfair price of Cleveland.

Start of match odds Cleveland 1.24.

Cleveland started well and were leading 33-19 after the first quarter. They carried on the good work to lead 63-48 at half time and were trading at 1.03.

Basketball is certainly a game where you should look to be laying at low prices early in the match; as this shows, Orlando made a magnificent comeback to win by 107-106.

Chennai v Punjab Indian Premier League Wednesday 20th May 2009

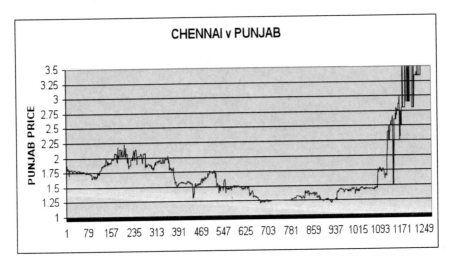

The chart represents the Betfair price of Punjab.

Start of match odds Punjab 1.78.

After bowling Chennai out for a below par score of 116, Punjab were strong favourites reaching 34 for one wicket after six overs and trading at 1.24.

They then went on to lose their next six wickets for 35 runs in their next 10 overs.

Never be afraid to lay a team who is chasing a low score as wickets change the price dramatically (as the above chart shows).

Think what is the worst thing that can happen in this scenario? A run chase is never easy under any circumstance.

Denver v LA Lakers 106–103 NBA Conference Finals Thursday 21st May 2009

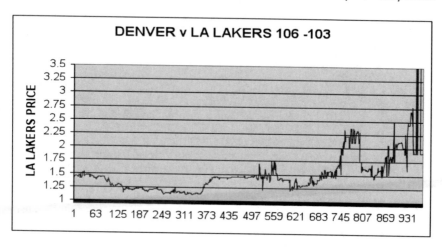

The chart represents the Betfair price of LA Lakers.

Start of match odds LA Lakers 1.42.

LA Lakers started the match positively, leading 31-23 in the first quarter. They then traded at 1.12 in the second quarter before going on to lose 106-103.

Once again, a classic example of laying a team who starts well early in the game.

So what can be concluded from this sample of six matches?

As previously stated, the preceding charts do not highlight a specific system, but what they do highlight is the danger of blindly backing low-priced favourites. You are far better waiting patiently for low laying opportunities to present themselves. The sporting markets present these opportunities on a daily basis. If you follow the right plan you can profit from them.

Just remember to keep on asking yourself the same question:

What is the worst thing that can happen if I place a lay bet at low odds in this scenario?

Rule 16: Take a contrarian view

Never blindly follow the money by backing low-priced favourites. There are many excellent low-risk trades available, if you take time and think outside the box.

20. Trading in Your Own Time Frame

I believe the subject of trading in a time frame that suits your own unique style is often overlooked.

Different time frames

It is hard enough profiting from a trading system, but to do this consistently you must be trading from within your own personal comfort zone. When you are experimenting with various trading systems you need to find one that gives you –

1. time to reach a decision, and

2. time to confidently act on that decision.

In other words, you need your decision-making process to be completely compatible with your natural time frame.

For example, when I was first introduced to Betfair I spent some time looking at pre-race trading the horse racing markets. In essence, these markets are no different to the pre-match under 2.5 goals markets that are discussed further on in this book. However, there is a huge difference in the time frame of the trades.

Completely differing time frames

Normally in the horse racing markets, trades are put on around 15 minutes before the race begins, and what follows can be a very quick roller coaster ride as the price moves up and down based on supply and demand.

Whereas, with the pre-match market on the football, I am often placing the trade the evening before the match; and generally the price moves sedately up until around 10 minutes before kick off. And when the price does get moving you know, well before, if you are on the right side of the trend.

Example of trading the wrong time frame

When I first started trading horse racing I suffered all sorts of problems.

First, I didn't know whether to back or lay a horse as I could not judge market sentiment. I was also hesitant about putting on a trade, even though I could see that the weight of money was on my side, because I had had previous bad experiences. This had two significant downsides.

1. If I was lucky enough to be on the right side of the trade, I was too quick to take a profit. As, due to the fast movement of the price, I was concerned that the price may rebound back past my entry point.

2. If a trade went against me, I sat paralysed hoping that the price would eventually turn and go my way, so I tended to suffer bigger losses than was really necessary.

Consequently, when I spent an afternoon trading the horses I won a little on quite a few races, broke even on a few, but my one or two large losses completely undid any previous good work.

I also finished the afternoon tired, exhausted and completely frustrated!

I am not saying that trading on horse racing should be avoided, as I know there are plenty of people who make a really substantial profit on a very regular basis. But what I am trying to highlight is that this particular market did and does not suit my own personal time frame.

I have since learned a lot about trading on horses, where many people use support and resistance in order to place and close their trades. But still, even if I followed this excellent advice, this market would still not suit my time frame.

Experiment and find your niche

I cannot say strongly enough that, if you are a beginner or relative newcomer to these markets, make sure that you experiment with as many markets as possible – because you will find your niche somewhere.

I believe that there are many potentially good traders out there who have been put off Betfair, and the betting exchanges in general, because they could not trade the horse racing markets successfully.

They presume they are a poor trader, but the probability is at that it didn't suit their personal time frame.

The problem is that a system may appear good, but once you put on the trade every other rule then goes out of the window, because time is probably the most important and underestimated element.

Going straight into quick-moving sporting markets can be extremely off putting. This in turn leads to hesitancy and reluctance to pull the trigger. This is another reason why you should always test a system thoroughly for a few months before committing any serious capital.

Obviously, finding a suitable market that matches your own personal time frame can be depend on many different factors, including:

- your temperament,

- your tolerance to risk,

- previous failure or success, and

- knowledge of the game.

If you are an individual who likes to think things through, then the pre-match football or test match cricket and golf are the best sports to trade.

On the other hand, if you are an impatient individual, the previous sports could leave you hungry for action and making wrong trades out of boredom, which will lead to inevitable losses.

Finally, it should be remembered that in each individual market, each individual trader is working to a completely different time frame. Some are scalping markets for a few ticks, whilst others are waiting patiently for various entry and exit points.

Rule 17: Trade within your individual time frame

Experiment in the markets and find the sports that are consistent with your natural time frame.

21. Balancing Trading and Living

I was going to deal with the next few topics separately:

1. Look after yourself.

2. Know when to take a break.

3. Withdraw your money regularly.

It was then that I realised that these three subjects are very much linked. This section of the book is about striking the right balance between your trading and your other interests and life responsibilities.

Betfair is and can be a very engrossing hobby, and unfortunately for many it can start occupying more time than maybe it should.

I have met many traders who are making the mistakes highlighted below – and have made many of these mistakes myself.

1. Look after yourself

Is this a familiar scenario?

Are you one of those individuals who wakes up in the morning and immediately switches on Sky Sports, closely followed by the computer, and then spends the next 12 to 15 hours slumped in front of the Betfair screen?

You then spend the day snacking on junk food, not getting dressed properly, or even opening the curtains. You then go to bed mentally exhausted, to repeat the same process all over again the next day.

If this sounds only too familiar, then you really need to address the situation and decide your reason for playing these markets. The behaviour described here is a recipe for disaster, and not only financially but physically and emotionally as well.

It takes discipline to succeed

The rules outlined in this book are in themselves quite easy to follow. However, they do take a tremendous amount of discipline to carry through. In order to succeed you have to be at the top of your game every single time you enter the market.

You therefore have to give yourself the chance to be the best you can.

Until recently I found myself making these very same mistakes. In my job I work away during the week, and spend the occasional weekend away from home. So as soon as I get home, I am looking to start trading. I found that I was going through the following bad habits.

Food

Although I was eating healthily during the day, I was certainly not taking time to eat properly in the evening.

The evening meal was a rushed affair, taken on the knee in front of the computer whilst trading.

And to ensure it didn't interrupt my time on the computer, it tended to be fattening, simple food like pizza. Also, if I was engrossed in what I was doing, the evening meal was often late in the evening, which didn't help when I was trying to get a good night's sleep.

Alcohol

After an evening of trading I tended to finish off around 10pm by opening a bottle of wine, and watching some TV programmes that I had recorded during the week. On many occasions this meant I was getting to bed at around 1am, and only having five hours of interrupted sleep. On some mornings I felt exhausted before the day had even started.

Exercise

Exercise just did not play a part in my life. I weighed around fifteen and a half stone and my waistline was increasing as the years went by.

Thankfully my line of work dictates that you have to be of a certain fitness level, and when I was not achieving this level it came as a big wake-up call. I have since addressed the situation.

Now, I am no expert on the subject of exercise, food and nutrition, but I soon worked out that I could not carry on living this type of lifestyle. I could also see that it was affecting my trading decisions, as I felt stale and devoid of energy.

So I set about making some simple changes.

Pre-plan your day

On rising in the morning I ensure that I plan out the events I am going to trade and the times I need to be by the computer, so that when it comes to the evening meal I am able to prepare it properly and eat it at a reasonable time.

I have joined a gym and ensure that I either go first thing in the morning, at lunchtime or straight after work. I also ensure that I do not drink any alcohol during the week, and I try to always ensure I have at least seven hours' sleep every night.

To start these new disciplines was quite difficult, especially keeping up an exercise plan. But today I can say that the work has paid off handsomely.

Not only am I now more awake and sharper during my trading, but my life is definitely more balanced. I would urge anyone who isn't doing so to try and make any or all of the small changes I mention above, as I believe you will, after six months or so, be astounded by the improvements.

2. Know when to take a break

Many new traders can become completely obsessed with trading the sporting markets.

Many feel compelled to be involved throughout the day in one market or another. For some individuals, the thought of not trading for a day is completely unpalatable.

The 24-hour market

Betfair is now becoming a 24-hour market. During the morning there can be various tennis tournaments starting around the world, in the afternoon there is the UK horse racing, in the evening there is football or cricket and later on, in the small hours of the morning, various sports from the USA take centre stage.

You can also trade via home or work PC, laptop and mobile phone whilst watching all the action live on various platforms.

It is therefore no surprise that a trader can very often become burnt out. Once you become stale, the act of trading becomes a real chore; and it is also at this time that you can start to lose discipline, and the strict rules you have been working to can quickly disappear.

As can the hard earned profits you have seen steadily grow in your account.

It can be at this stage that many traders forget the real reason they are trading. For many the reason to trade is to give them more income so they can enjoy other areas of their life that are important to them.

You have to be the best you can

Unfortunately trading in the Betfair markets is not like some professions or jobs, where you only have to turn up and put in an average performance in order to pick up your pay slip.

On these markets you have to be the best you possibly can be, on top of your game each and every day; otherwise the probability is you will lose money.

To stay at your best it is imperative that you plan to take regular time out away from the markets, and take adequate rest and recuperation to recharge the batteries.

When you do take a break, ensure that it is a complete break away from the markets – when you go away for the weekend or on holiday, ensure that you leave the laptop at home!

A good break helps you clear your head and gain a fresh perspective on things, and it will certainly help improve your overall performance.

You are not going to miss anything by leaving the markets alone for a few days. There will always be another tennis or golf tournament, or cricket match, starting in the next few days.

Plan the events to trade well in advance

One of the advantages of having a second diary is that you can highlight the sporting fixtures throughout the coming months that you are going to trade. It means you can then decide beforehand the days and weeks you are going to take off.

For example, if your specialisation is Twenty20 cricket, a good time to take a break would be straight after the Indian Premier League or straight after the World Cup.

Only you yourself know if your trading is starting to decline, but once you feel that your performance is starting to suffer, then that is the time to take a break.

3. Withdraw money regularly

Regular withdrawals of money from your Betfair account can be very healthy for your trading, especially if you are withdrawing your money and putting it towards something that is personally rewarding to yourself.

It is extremely important that you do not fall into the trap of building up money in your account just for the sake of it.

Decide the level you are happy trading at, and ensure the rest of your money is away from your Betfair account and working for you.

As an example, some traders are happy trading at a certain level and they just cannot emotionally adjust to increasing their stakes. I personally like trading at a certain stake size and I believe this helps me to trade as well as possible.

Decide your financial goals

Another thing that is often overlooked by traders is that you should always have a financial goal to work towards.

I would suggest that if you have no financial goal, you take some time out and decide what you want to achieve by trading the Betfair markets. One of my personal goals is to pay for my holidays. For some people they would just be happy to win enough money to pay for their internet and satellite television.

Personal goals:

- Give you a real reason to be involved in the market.
- Keep you more focused.
- Help you stay on track and disciplined in your approach.

Do not become attached to your trading bank

One of the downsides of not withdrawing money is that just by growing your trading account you then start becoming attached to the money.

This can lead to many mistakes, such as chasing losses and trading out of fear. You have to ask yourself:

What good is this large amount of money doing in my account?

I met a client who was obsessed with growing his bank just for the sake of trading with larger sums of money. He had a system where he liked to lay golfers in the final round of a tournament. When he was staking up to £3 a tick he was doing fine. But once he started increasing his stakes to £5 or more he simply fell apart. This gentleman was a successful businessman and had also made some very good financial investments, so could easily afford to lose the money; but he could not adjust to increasing his stake size.

A means to an end

Money is basically a means to an end and a tool to allow you to do and enjoy all the good things in life, so ensure that you use it to its full potential by making regular withdrawals from your account.

I hope this section has given you something to think about, and hopefully you will keep your trading in perspective and find your own balance in life, realising that there is more to life than just trading the sporting markets.

Rule 18: Always keep your trading in perspective

 Keep your trading in perspective and find your own balance in life. Realise that there is more to life than just trading the sporting markets.

PART FIVE

Strategies

22. Introduction

In this section of the book I am going to introduce you to a number of strategies that you can start using in the markets. The beauty about many of these strategies is that they –

1. are not set in stone, and

2. can be altered to suit your own style.

The only strategy that suggests employing a mechanical trading system is the tennis strategy (although you can make slight changes to this strategy if you so desire).

These strategies have been developed as a result of several years of research. I strongly believe that, should you really want to be successful, you need to specialise and know your sport inside out – in other words, you need to put the work in.

Overreaction in the markets

In the following you will hear a lot about how markets overreact. Before I go on to present the strategies, I would like to explain how overreaction occurs in these markets and how we can profit from it.

Every sport has significant moments during the game. For example, in golf, when a birdie put is sunk; in cricket, when a wicket is taken or a boundary is hit; in tennis, when a serve is broken; and obviously, in football, when a goal is scored.

When these events occur there is usually an overreaction in the market. For example, when a wicket is taken in a cricket match. The price of the batting team can rise suddenly from 1.20 to 1.45 when in reality the correct price should be 1.38.

This happens frequently in tennis. A player who breaks serve can go from 1.50 to 1.20, when the price should be nearer 1.25.

It is in these moments that I am looking to exploit these prices. This is the area in which many of my strategies have been created. The strategies are generally low risk, where you are opposing a low-priced favourite – where there is very little down side and much to gain.

Find your ideal market

There is no question about the fact that it is a big advantage if you are very knowledgeable and have a keen interest in the sport you are looking to trade. However, as previously stated, it is not a good idea to trade a match or event in which you will become emotionally involved. For example, I never trade a football match in which my favourite team is playing as it can cloud my judgement.

Also, don't start trading a sport just because others are doing so. If you have no interest in what you are trading, you will probably lose; and it will certainly show up in your profitability.

You cannot and must not let others decide where your passion lies. I would suggest you follow your gut feeling and find the market that speaks out to you, and then fully immerse yourself in the market.

When you are passionate about a subject, this helps with your competence in reading the markets and, indeed, following your chosen market can become more of a calling than a learning exercise. There is no better feeling than knowing you are beating the market because of your new-found knowledge and skills.

It also helps if you understand your psychological make up. As mentioned in a previous chapter, you need to be happy with the time frame in which you have chosen to trade. For example, if you like to think things through then the strategy for the tennis tournament or the pre-match under/over 2.5 goal strategy will suit you. If you like making fast decisions, then the Twenty20 cricket and tennis strategies may be best for you. Either way, it is important that you feel comfortable in your trading.

You then need to go through the following process.

1. Experiment with the strategies to find an edge.

2. Stake yourself correctly.

3. Follow the system with confidence, avoiding extreme emotional highs and lows.

4. Focus on executing your trading system correctly for each trade you place in the market.

Remember it is not about the profitability of individual trades, but the consistent results of weeks and months of trading that counts. At the end of each day or week you should evaluate and improve your system.

23. Football

Football is an extremely popular sport to trade on Betfair. What follows are a few examples of the most popular trading strategies.

> Of the strategies presented below, I only ever use the underdog strategy and the pre-match trading of the under 2.5 goals.

Trading the erosion of time

Trading time erosion is where you are looking to nip in and out of the market extremely quickly, taking the odd tick here and there as the price erodes due to time passing by in the match.

For example, a match between Liverpool and Chelsea might be a draw with 30 minutes remaining, at which time the odds for the draw will be priced around 2.10. Should the game remain a draw, the price erodes extremely quickly – as in the following example.

Example of match Liverpool v Chelsea drawing after 60 minutes

Minute	61	64	66	69	71	74
Price	2.10	2.02	1.93	1.84	1.76	1.67
Minute	76	78	81	83	86	
Price	1.58	1.50	1.41	1.33	1.23	

The ideal scenario in this case would be around the 70-minute mark, when a player goes down injured requiring a substitution. In this scenario, after the play has stopped and the time is ticking by, the price could fall from around 1.75 to 1.67 in a couple of minutes, leaving you with a nice 8-tick profit.

Underdog taking the lead

On a Saturday afternoon on Betfair, the Premiership matches are in-play and I am always on the lookout for early shock scores.

Take the following example of a match I traded.

Example: Fulham v Arsenal (final score 2–1)

Fulham went into a 2-0 lead after 19 minutes and were then priced at 1.37 to win the match. I immediately layed for £100, hoping for a quick Arsenal come back. So my exposure was £37 to win £100.

Arsenal then went on the offensive, putting Fulham under intense pressure, before going on to score in the 36th minute.

This then raised the Fulham price to 2.06, resulting in an immediate 69-tick profit, which, when greened up, meant I had profited by £33 no matter what the result of the match.

I had nearly an hour of the game left for Arsenal to close the gap and secure a profit of £100.

Alternative strategy

Another strategy would have been to let the bet run for 40 minutes in the hope that Arsenal would have equalised or, indeed, taken the lead. Providing the score remained the same, Fulham would not have hit 1.37 again until around the 75th minute.

However, as it happened, the score remained 2–1, and Fulham could quite easily have extended their lead. When trading in a scenario like the above, I always advise taking profit at the earliest opportunity.

Trade analysis

I knew, at 2-0 down, Arsenal were going to do all that they could to get back into the game. And so it proved by them scoring. However, once that goal was scored, the approach to the match can change from both sides. So I always prefer to exit the trade as soon as the profit presents itself.

As you can see, there was so much to gain by the above scenario. I was risking a relatively minimal sum, compared to what could have been won. I was backing a team to come back, who on paper were stronger and who very much needed to win.

All of the right ingredients were in place to set up a very good trade. Had Fulham scored a third goal and gone 3-0 up then I would have lost £37. However, even at 2-0 the price would not have gone down by all that much until the final 15 minutes of the match – and I had an hour for Arsenal (one of the best sides in the league) to get back into the match, which is exactly what happened.

Pre-match over/under 2.5 goals

This is one of my favourite markets and a market that I trade regularly. This strategy has proved successful over the past few years.

We will look at a Manchester United v Everton match as an example.

Example: Manchester United v Everton

The current overs/unders 2.5 goals market shows the following odds (Figure 5.1).

Figure 5.1: Odds available Manchester United v Everton

Man Utd v Everton - Over/Under 2.5 goals ⊞						
☐ Going in-play 🔟 Live Scores					Matched: GBP 24,409 [Refresh]	
☑ Back & Lay ☑ Market Depth					More options ▶	
Selections: (2)	100.7%		**Back**	**Lay**		99.6%
ılıl **Under 2.5 Goals**	1.77 £3	1.79 £135	**1.81** £105	**1.82** £185	1.83 £915	1.84 £1954
ılıl **Over 2.5 Goals**	2.16 £682	2.18 £1691	**2.2** £854	**2.24** £47	2.28 £117	2.38 £80

Stage 1

When analysing these markets I am looking at each team's strengths and weaknesses, goals scored home and away etc, and assessing if the game will be low scoring. I refer to various websites and newspapers such as the *Racing Post*.

At this stage I am doing my research and trying to gauge market sentiment.

I then turn to the spread betting website www.sportingindex.com, I scroll down and on the left-hand side look under "SPORTS" for the various Football options, in this section you will find the match you are after. Click into the game and look at the Total Goals tab. On going down to this tab I see that they are selling 2.40 goals and buying 2.60 goals (Figure 5.2).

Figure 5.2: Sporting Index total goals market

MAN UTD V EVERTON

Bets > Football UK (TV) > Man Utd v Everton

FA Cup Semi-Final (Played at Wembley)
Sunday 19th April. Live on ITV1 at 16.00.
Note: All markets are 90 minutes play only.
Player goal minutes will be updated 'in-play'.

Market	So far	Price	Stake	Action	
Man Utd/Everton	0-0	0.7 - 0.9		SELL	BUY
Total Goals	0	2.4 - 2.6		SELL	BUY
Shirt Numbers	0	37 - 40		SELL	BUY
Shirt Supremacy: M U/Eve	0-0	11 - 14		SELL	BUY
Corners	0	10.5 - 11		SELL	BUY
Corner Supremacy: M U/Eve	0-0	1.75 - 2.75		SELL	BUY
Bookings	0	46 - 50		SELL	BUY
Booking Supremacy: Eve/M U (h)	0-0	5 - 9		SELL	BUY
Man Utd Win Index		15.5 - 17		SELL	BUY
Everton Win Index		6.5 - 8		SELL	BUY
Hotshots	0	30 - 33		SELL	BUY
Total Goal Minutes	0	120 - 130		SELL	BUY
TGMs Supremacy: M U/Eve	0-0	33 - 47		SELL	BUY
Multi-Corners	0x0	27.5 - 30.5		SELL	BUY

DISABLE AUTO UPDATES

To find out how many goals the spread firms believe will be in this game, you simply add the 'sell total goals' to the 'buy total goals' and divide by 2. In this example it is:

```
2.4 + 2.6 = 5.0
```

```
5.0/2 = 2.5
```

This means that this spread firm believe there will be 2.5 goals scored in this match. I also check the IG Index spread betting website to see what they are suggesting the total goals will be. Usually they are quoting the same spread, but occasionally there is a difference.

Stage 2

Below is a table which represents the predicted Betfair odds for goal expectation. These odds are derived from the statistics gained from thousands of previous matches, and are regarded as the accepted odds in the betting industry.

Goal expectation	Odds under 2.5 goals	Odds over 2.5 goals
2.2	1.60	2.66
2.3	1.68	2.50
2.4	1.75	2.34
2.5	1.84	2.22
2.6	1.92	2.09
2.7	2.02	1.99
2.8	2.12	1.89
2.9	2.24	1.82
3.0	2.35	1.74
3.1	2.48	1.68
3.2	2.61	1.62

I look at the table and find the corresponding price. In this case it would be *Goal expectation 2.5* and in this case the under price is 1.84 and the Over price is 2.22. It therefore suggests that this market is about correct; but based on the current price traders believe the price could move nearer to the *Goal expectation 2.4* price of 1.75. rather than move out to the *Goal expectation 2.6* price of 1.92.

Stage 3

I then go to the website www.oddschecker.com and check the prices the other firms are offering for the under 2.5 goals market.

In the highlighted Manchester United v Everton match there were the following quotes from various bookmakers (Figure 5.3).

Figure 5.3: Bookmaker quotes from Oddschecker for Manchester United v Everton

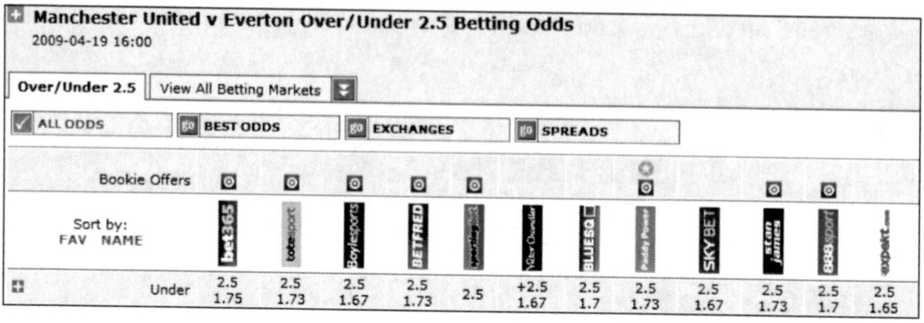

Manchester United v Everton Over/Under 2.5 Betting Odds
2009-04-19 16:00

Over/Under 2.5 | View All Betting Markets

ALL ODDS | BEST ODDS | EXCHANGES | SPREADS

Sort by: FAV NAME	bet365	totesport	Boylesports	BETFRED		Victor Chandler	BLUESQ		SKYBET	stan james	888sport	expekt
Under	2.5 1.75	2.5 1.73	2.5 1.67	2.5 1.73	2.5	+2.5 1.67	2.5 1.7	2.5 1.73	2.5 1.67	2.5 1.73	2.5 1.7	2.5 1.65

We can now conclude from what the other firms are offering that if we back on this market at the current price of 1.81, we are not making a horrendous error – as the bookmakers are only offering prices ranging between 1.65 and 1.75.

Finally I do a quick calculation by seeing how many games have featured less than under 2.5 goals in their previous 20 matches, related to whether or not they are home or away to calculate the odds.

Note: in this example the match is played at Wembley, so I am basing the following on both team's away form.

- In Manchester United's last 20 away games, they had: **13 matches** ending in under 2.5 goals.

- In Everton's last 20 away games they had: **13 matches** ending in under 2.5 goals.

This left a total of 26 games out of 40 ending in under 2.5 goals.

I then do the following calculation.

26 games ending under 2.5 goals divided by the 40 matches, multiplied by 100, equals 65. This 65 represents the percentage probability of under 2.5 goals being scored (on historic form). I then divide 100 by 65, which gives the odds of 1.54.

So, according to the previous 40 matches these two teams were involved in, the true price for under 2.5 goals should be around 1.54. This would indicate that the current odds of 1.81/1.82 (available at Betfair) are offering reasonable value.

Value

I would just like to briefly touch on the subject of value by saying *value* is based on your own individual perception. It is not an exact science.

The reason I felt that this particular trade offered value was because I was looking to back under 2.5 goals at 1.81, which represents a 55% (100/1.81) chance as opposed to the 1.54 (65%) chance based on the statistics of the two team's previous 20 matches.

Other traders may use other methods to derive value. For example, they may look at just the last 10 matches. They may also look at previous matches between the two sides (head to head encounters). It is very much an individual preference, but, for the purposes of this strategy, looking at the two team's last 10 to 20 matches will give you a reasonable indication as to whether you are gaining any value or not.

Stage 4

I then use the odds comparison chart (which can be found in the Appendix), and decide which price offers the best value.

In these markets I tend to trade at £5 a tick, but am not prepared to accept the current price of 1.81 on offer as experience says I may get 1.82 or better.

I do not place my money (£500 backing at 1.82) as it will then appear on the lay side. Instead I consult the chart on page 129 and decide to –

Lay over 2.5 goals for £409.84 at 2.22 (which is the same as backing under 2.5 goals for £500 at the price of 1.82) (Figure 5.4).

Figure 5.4: Placing £409.84 lay bet on Over 2.5 goals at 2.22

The reason I do this is that many more punters prefer to straight back a selection, meaning my bet will get taken early.

If I was to place my £500 in the under 2.5 goal market at 1.82, it then gets placed on the lay side and you are left hoping that someone lays your bet.

 It is far easier for someone to back your selection than to lay it, and there are many more customers on Betfair who prefer to back a selection than lay a selection.

I am therefore in the position of showing a potential profit of £409.84 on under 2.5 goals, and a liability of £500 on over 2.5 goals (Figure 5.5).

Figure 5.5: Potential profit and liability

Man Utd v Everton - Over/Under 2.5 goals ⊞							
☐ Going in-play Ⅲ Live Scores					Matched: GBP 24,641 Refresh		
☑ Back & Lay ☑ Market Depth					More options ▸		
Selections: (2)	100.7%		**Back**	**Lay**		99.6%	
ⅲ **Under 2.5 Goals** » £409.84	1.79 £135	1.8 £8	1.81 £57	1.82 £179	1.83 £915	1.84 £1954	
ⅲ **Over 2.5 Goals** » -£500.00	2.16 £2056	2.18 £1691	2.2 £805	2.24 £47	2.28 £117	2.38 £80	

I then place the bet and (as you can see from Figure 5.6) my £409 lay bet has now been placed in the market on the back side.

Figure 5.6: £409.84 lay bet at 2.22 enters the market on the back side

Man Utd v Everton - Over/Under 2.5 goals ⊞							
☐ Going in-play Ⅲ Live Scores					Matched: GBP 24,641 Refresh		
☑ Back & Lay ☑ Market Depth					More options ▸		
Selections: (2)	100.3%		**Back**	**Lay**		99.6%	
ⅲ **Under 2.5 Goals**	1.79 £95	1.8 £8	1.81 £57	1.82 £179	1.83 £915	1.84 £1954	
ⅲ **Over 2.5 Goals**	2.18 £1691	2.2 £1393	2.22 £409	2.24 £47	2.26 £60	2.28 £34	

When I place my money in this particular market I am always looking to make at least 2.5% on any trade, which means in this case I am looking to make at least £12.50.

In order to make my 2.5% I am putting in the following orders: I am laying under 2.5 goals for £514.00 at 1.77 which, if hit, will give me a profit of £14.00, no matter what the result (Figures 5.7 & 5.8).

Figure 5.7: Laying Under 2.5 goals at 1.77

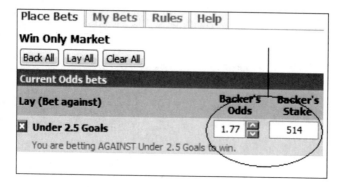

Figure 5.8: Potential profit of £14.00 on both results should bet at 1.77 be matched

Man Utd v Everton - Over/Under 2.5 goals ⊕						
☐ Going in-play ⊞ Live Scores				Matched: GBP 26,421 [Refresh]		
☑ Back & Lay ☑ Market Depth						More options ▶
Selections: (2)	100.9%		**Back**	**Lay**		99.5%
ᵢᵢᵢ Under 2.5 Goals £409.84 ≈ £14.06	1.75 £1162	1.77 £3	1.79 £170	1.81 £26	1.82 £120	1.83 £920
ᵢᵢᵢ Over 2.5 Goals -£500.00 ≈ £14.00	2.18 £1691	2.2 £1374	2.22 £20	2.26 £85	2.28 £34	2.38 £80

As you can see, this would only take a 5 tick movement from 1.82 to 1.77 in order for a profit to be made. And indeed, a few hours later the trade was filled and a £14 profit was made (Figure 5.9). As you can see, I could have left this trade in the market and have been matched at 1.75 or below.

Figure 5.9: A £14 profit is secured by the bet being matched at 1.77

Man Utd v Everton - Over/Under 2.5 goals ⊕						
☐ Going in-play ⊞ Live Scores				Matched: GBP 87,205 [Refresh]		
☑ Back & Lay ☑ Market Depth						More options ▶
Selections: (2)	100.6%		**Back**	**Lay**		99.2%
ᵢᵢᵢ Under 2.5 Goals £14.06	1.73 £3906	1.74 £388	1.75 £1202	1.77 £5957	1.78 £377	1.8 £728
ᵢᵢᵢ Over 2.5 Goals £14.00	2.26 £395	2.28 £178	2.3 £375	2.34 £438	2.36 £87	2.38 £80

You would be amazed the number of times these orders get filled, and a profit is secured before the game kicks off.

Note: I am using 2.5% profit just as an example; between 5 and 10% gains are easily possible in these markets – especially when the price moves just before kick off.

Stage 5

I always tend to place my stop loss at the price relating to the spread betting companies' buying point. In this example it was 2.6 goals, which relates to a price of 1.92.

Trading the national team

England are excellent to trade in this market (especially against so-called weaker opposition) because punters overrate their chances and goal scoring ability.

England are also very good in this market because they actually concede very few goals.

I have made a substantial profit in recent seasons trading pre-kick-off in matches against Greece, Macedonia and Croatia. In fact, on two occasions I made over 7% of my bank, and this was well before the game had kicked off.

24. Tennis

Trading the favourites during tournament progression

Predicting the shift in odds in knockout competitions can be extremely profitable, and lends itself excellently to tennis tournaments.

The odds on at least one competitor winning a tournament will always be 100%. However, as the tournament progresses and the number of competitors falls, so do the odds of the remaining competitors, and the 100% gets redistributed as each round is completed.

For example, should someone trading at 4.0 be knocked out of a competition, then there is 25% of probability that needs to be redistributed throughout the rest of the remaining competitors.

Look for the favourite to progress early

This strategy lends itself very well to tennis, as competitors are always being knocked out at differing times during the tournament. Sometimes different competitors can be knocked out of the same round on different days.

Your strategy would be to look for one of the favourites to progress to the next round early, whilst his close rivals are still to play (it also helps if the player concerned has a relatively easy next round). You then back this player. If any of his rivals should be knocked out of the competition, then the price on the player you have backed will fall significantly. And even if all of his close rivals do progress, the price will only drift ever so slightly.

This is an excellent low risk strategy, as the following example shows.

Trading tournament example

Nikolay Davydenko was priced at 10.5 (9.52% chance of winning) third favourite for a very open tournament in Paris. He had already qualified for the third round and all his close rivals were still to play in the second round.

So I backed him for £50. Inevitably a couple of his rivals lost and his price went down to 8.0 (12.5% chance of winning). He was due to play the next round first and was a hot favourite priced around 1.2.

I figured he would still progress further and his odds would shorten dramatically; so to protect my position I layed him for £50 at 1.2 during this match. Which then meant, if he went out, I would lose nothing.

He duly won and I lost £10. However, his price to win the tournament then went down to 5 (20% chance of winning tournament). Obviously I let this bet stand as, once again, all his rivals were yet to play, and yet again a close rival lost and his price again down further to 3.25 (30% chance of winning).

It was then that I greened up to ensure a £110 profit whoever won. This ended up being a £100 profit as I had lost £10 during the earlier lay.

Always keep an eye on match timings

As you can see, providing you do your homework and keep an eye on the times the matches take place (all this information is available on the atptennis.com website), this strategy can prove to be extremely profitable with very low risk.

Obviously this strategy can work for any tournament in any sport. For example, should a team like Manchester United get through to the next round of the FA Cup in a lunchtime kick off before everybody else is set to play, it might be worth backing them in the hope that one or more of their main rivals such as Chelsea, Liverpool and Arsenal lose that afternoon.

Trading tournament graphic example

As an example of how you can benefit from trading a tournament, we will look at the following example.

Andy Roddick has already progressed to the semi-final and will play Tommy Haas.

Fernando Gonzalez has also progressed to the semi-final stage and will play the winner of the only other outstanding quarter-final match which is Juan Del Porto v Tomas Berdych.

As we can see from Table 1, Andy Roddick is the favourite at 2.02 and Juan del Porto is also heavily fancied to beat Tomas Berdych and progress to the final.

Table 5.1: The tournament prices at quarter-final stage of ATP event

PLAYER	BACK	% CHANCE of WINNING
Andy Roddick	2.02	49.72
Juan Del Porto	3.20	31.25
Fernando Gonzalez	7.00	14.28
Tommy Haas	28.00	3.57
Tomas Berdych	36.00	2.77
TOTAL PERCENTAGE		101.59

At the moment, Andy Roddick's price is based on the probability that he will be facing Juan Del Porto in the final.

As Andy Roddick has already gone through to the semi-final, now is a good time to back him.

Juan Del Porto is priced at 1.20 (83.33%) to beat Tomas Berdych, who is priced at 6.0 (16.66%).

So the scenario is as follows.

There is a 16.67% chance that Del Porto will lose this match.

Should he lose, then Andy Roddick's price will plummet, as the 31.25% chance of Juan Del Porto winning this tournament will have to be distributed around the other competitors.

On the down side, should Juan Del Porto win the match, then Andy Roddick's price may move out a few ticks, but this would be minimal.

The reason for this is that Andy Roddick's price has already factored in that Del Porto will win this match and probably face him in the final.

As we can see from Table 5.2, Tomas Berdych beat Juan Del Porto and Andy Roddick's price went down to 1.60.

Table 5.2: The Tournament prices at semi-final stage

PLAYER	BACK	% CHANCE of WINNING
Andy Roddick	1.60	62.50
Fernando Gonzalez	5.00	20.00
Tomas Berdych	9.00	11.11
Tommy Haas	13.00	7.69
TOTAL PERCENTAGE		101.30

As you can see, by backing Andy Roddick you would have made a handsome profit for very little risk.

However, be warned – unless the tournament is high profile, liquidity can be a problem, and it is unlikely that you would be able to place large amounts of money in the market.

On the other hand, if you use this system for trading a football tournament such as the Champions League, then this is not a problem. This strategy lends itself particularly well to tennis because of the different times matches take place, and it is not unusual for a favourite to be beaten by a big outsider.

Back-testing a strategy

Recently I have been looking at various ways of playing the tennis market by laying at low prices, mainly concentrating on what happens once the favourite's price dips below 1.10.

The initial strategy enjoyed a modicum of success, but the profits were not as consistent as I would have liked them to be.

I analysed over 900 matches of data which was split between women's and men's three set matches. All the data that follows refers to the three set games.

As I trawled through the data it soon became apparent that the favourite's price rose above the starting price (SP) a significant number of times. By SP I mean the last available lay price before the match went in-play.

As you can see from the table below, of the 906 matches analysed in 784, or 86.5% of matches, the price rose above the SP.

Table 5.3: Analysis of favourites' Starting Prices

Starting Price	Times Above SP	Times Below SP	No of Matches	% of Matches That Go Above SP
2.00-1.00	784	122	906	86.5%

I felt that this in its own way was significant, but now I had to figure out how to turn this data into a profitable system.

Note: This research is still ongoing. If you would like a copy of the Excel spreadsheet please e-mail me at masteringbetfair@petenordsted.com.

Use the data to produce your own strategies

Obviously the main analysis Excel spreadsheet can be filtered and manipulated to suit and try out different strategies. But the strategy outlined below will give you a good start, and is an excellent example of the type of systems you should be looking to implement in your trading plan.

The four tables presented below highlight which matches within a set price range produce the most occasions when the favourite at some stage trades above his or her starting price.

For example, with reference to the first table, look at the first row in this table.

- The first column highlights those matches where the favourite's starting price was between 1.10 and 1.00.

- The second column highlights the number of matches that the favourite traded above his/her starting price. In this example it is 77.

- The third column highlights the number of matches that the favourite did *not* trade above his/her starting price. In this example it is 28.

- The fourth column indicates the number of matches that were analysed. In this example it is 105.

- The fifth column indicates the percentage of those matches that the favourite traded above the starting price.

This then gives you an indication as to the area and price range where there is the most chance of a favourite trading above their starting price.

If you look at the tables below and go down to the 30 tick spread table you will see (the shaded row) the starting price is 1.50 – 1.21.

As you can see, out of 416 matches 376 (90.3%) at some stage the price of the favourite rose above the SP.

Table 5.4: 10 tick spread

Starting price	Times Above SP	Times Below SP	No of Matches	% of Matches That Go Above SP
1.10-1.00	77	28	105	73.3%
1.20-1.11	71	16	87	81.6%
1.30-1.21	79	10	89	88.7%
1.40-1.31	91	9	100	91.0%
1.50-1.41	68	6	74	91.9%
1.60-1.51	72	11	83	86.7%
1.70-1.61	66	8	74	89.2%
1.80-1.71	39	6	45	86.6%
1.90-1.81	34	1	35	97.1%
2.00-1.91	27	3	30	90.0%

Table 5.5: 20 tick spread

Starting Price	Times Above SP	Times Below SP	No of Matches	% of Matches That Go Above SP
1.20-1.00	148	44	192	77.0%
1.30-1.11	150	26	176	85.2%
1.40-1.21	170	19	189	89.9%
1.50-1.31	159	15	174	91.4%
1.60-1.41	140	17	157	89.2%
1.70-1.51	138	19	157	87.9%
1.80-1.61	105	14	119	88.2%
1.90-1.71	72	7	79	91.1%
2.00-1.81	61	4	65	93.8%

Table 5.6: 30 tick spread

Starting Price	Times Above SP	Times Below SP	No of Matches	% of Matches That Go Above SP
1.30-1.00	227	54	281	80.7%
1.40-1.11	241	35	276	87.3%
1.50-1.21	376	40	416	90.3%
1.60-1.31	231	26	257	91.1%
1.70-1.41	206	25	231	89.1%
1.80-1.51	177	25	202	87.6%
1.90-1.61	139	15	154	90.2%
2.00-1.71	100	10	110	90.9%

Table 5.7: 40 tick spread

Starting Price	Times Above SP	Times Below SP	No of Matches	% of Matches That Go Above SP
1.40-1.00	318	63	381	83.4%
1.50-1.11	309	41	350	88.3%
1.60-1.21	310	36	346	89.6%
1.70-1.31	297	34	331	89.7%
1.80-1.41	245	31	276	88.8%
1.90-1.51	211	26	237	89.0%
2.00-1.61	166	18	184	90.2%

Tennis strategies

Note: The accompanying tables for the two strategies we are looking to use on tennis appear in the appendices. This is where you will also find an example of trading strategy 2 (back at 1.50) over a month.

Strategy 1: back at 2.0

On looking at the matches where the favourite SP was between 1.50 and 1.21.

We are going to –

1. lay £100 at 1.25, and then

2. lay a further £200 at 1.13 should the price go down.

I have highlighted what happens when you –

1. back at 2.00 and

2. green up at 2.00.

In this example, the price hit the lay price of 1.25 (or SP below 1.25) 305 times.

1. Of the 305 matches, 159 of the matches did not reach the target price of 2.00. If we had layed £100 on each selection at 1.25, and a further £200 at 1.13, we would have lost £6209.

2. 146 of the matches after laying at 1.25 and 1.13 went on to hit the target price of 2.00. If you had greened up at 2.00, this would have produced £13,059 (or £12,406 after deducting 5% commission). This would have produced £6197 profit (£12,406 - £6209).

3. Of the 146 Matches that hit 2.0 after laying at 1.25, and 1.13 after backing to win at 2.0, 75 went on to win and 71 went on to lose. This would have produced £13,309 (or £12,644 after deducting 5% commission). This would have produced £6435 profit (£12,644 - £6209).

Strategy 2: back at 1.5

On looking at the matches where the favourite's SP was between 1.50 and 1.21.

We are going to –

1. lay £100 at 1.25, and then

2. lay a further £200 at 1.13 should the price go down.

I have highlighted what happens when you –

1. back at 1.50, and

2. green up at 1.50.

In this example, the price hit the lay price of 1.25 (or SP below 1.25) 305 times.

1. Of the 305 matches, 101 of the matches did not reach the target price of 1.50. If we had layed £100 on each selection at 1.25, and a further £200 at 1.13, we would have lost £4074.

2. 204 of the matches after laying at 1.25 and 1.13 went on to hit the target price of 1.50. If you had greened up at 1.50, this would have produced £9112 (or £8656 after deducting 5% commission). This would have produced a £4582 profit (£8656 - £4074).

3. Of the 204 Matches that hit 1.50 after laying at 1.25 and 1.13 after backing to win at 2.0, 133 went onto win and 71 went on to lose. This would have produced £8719 (or £8283 after deducting 5% commission). Which would have produced £8283 - £4074 = £4209 profit.

The strategy rules

So the rule would be: if the SP is between 1.50 – 1.21:

1. Lay as soon as price hits 1.25 providing this is done during the first set of the match. Preferably you should be laying when the price just goes straight down to the 1.25 level from the SP.

2. If the price goes further down to 1.13, double your lay, then either back at 2.00 or 1.50 and green up or leave.

Losses could be reduced further by setting a stop loss after the price has risen above the SP. In the example, a stop loss has been set at 1.10, but remember that this is only done once the price goes above the SP.

This strategy could also be adjusted with the following rules.

1. If the price goes up 10 ticks from the SP before coming down to the 1.25 level then **no bet**.

2. Also, if the price goes over 10 ticks above the SP, then comes back down, stop loss at the price you entered (i.e. the SP) rather than wait out to stop at 1.10.

25. Twenty20 Cricket

There is no doubt that the Twenty20 version of the game has revolutionised cricket and the format looks as though it is here to stay. At the moment I don't believe enough matches have been played to devise a mechanical plan for trading, but with the Indian Premier League and the World Cup, combined with the introduction of the English league, by 2010 there should be enough data available to see if any obvious patterns emerge.

However, presented below is a list of strategies that can be employed during the matches which should prove profitable.

1st innings trading opportunities

Three trading ideas:

1. If the **batting side get off to a flying start** then the best time to lay them would be after around three-seven overs, when the team batting are priced between 1.30 – 1.50.

2. If the **bowling side take a few early wickets** in the first ten overs then look to lay them between odds of 1.30 – 1.50. In the Twenty20 version of the game, wickets are of less importance as the batsman only have to play 20 overs. Also, it only takes a couple of players to come to the crease and hit 20 to 30 runs in one over to completely change the direction of the game.

3. These matches also present some excellent low-risk trading opportunities when there is a **strong pre-match favourite** playing, especially if they are priced between 1.40 – 1.60. This is because if the favourite makes a strong start, either batting or bowling, their odds will shorten very rapidly. This then makes for a good low lay trade, as in this format of cricket every team has an equal chance to win.

2nd innings trading opportunities

Two trading ideas:

1. For a **high run chase** scenario, where the first innings score is between 170-210, if the batting team start well, after around seven-ten overs then look to lay at low odds between 1.20 – 1.40. Also, if the bowling team have taken early wickets, look to lay at low odds between 1.10 – 1.30.

2. For a **low run chase** scenario where the first innings score is between 110-140, if the batting team start well, after around two-five overs look to lay at low odds between 1.01 – 1.20. Also, if the batting team start poorly and lose some early wickets then look to back them at the higher odds between 1.60 – 1.80.

The best time to lay

Below are highlighted the best scenarios for laying a team. Also, always try to take momentum/overreaction odds (i.e. after boundaries or wickets).

1st innings laying opportunities

1. Look to **lay the batting team** after a flying start in low odds (1.30) in the first five overs, or after four-five wickets, when odds are around 1.25 – 1.30 in middle overs.

2. Look to **lay the bowling team** when it has taken up to three wickets and the odds are around 1.30 in the first ten overs.

2nd innings laying opportunities

1. **Low run chase:** Wait for batting team to be between 1.01 and 1.10 after two wickets. Even after two wickets the odds are still the same as at the start but the chances of a large drift in price is far greater after two wickets have fallen.

2. **High run chase:** Wait for the batting team to hit around 1.30. Lay if making a good start in a high chase match.

Here are a couple of points that should always be remembered when you are considering laying at low odds:

1. Wickets are of less importance in this format of the game, so consider laying the bowling team if it has taken wickets and the price is between 1.30 – 1.40 in first ten overs.

2. If the match is played by two teams of equal ability, then you should always lay at odds between 1.20 – 1.30 if this comes early in the match, as one good over by the batting or bowling side can shift the odds dramatically up.

Volatile market strategy

Obviously, in this format of cricket there is every possibility that you could have a very volatile market in each match. I believe it is best to avoid trading at this time.

Never ever back a team at low odds in these scenarios.

I always like to trade early in a match and leave the game alone once a profit is secured.

If you really must trade, then I would suggest a small lay of any team at 1.20 or below. There are three benefits to this strategy:

1. If the trade goes against us, then the loss is small because we have layed at short odds.

2. We have a lot to gain and very little to lose. So the profit expectancy is large.

3. The most important benefit is you can close this trade easily any time. For example, if you have layed £100 at 1.22, then there is plenty of time and plenty of opportunities to back at 1.14 – 1.18 to trade out for a very small loss.

Also in high volatile situations always try to side with the bowling team in a tense situation and lay the batting team at between 1.10 – 1.20.

Advance lay/back plans and stop loss

As with most other trading, it is important that you have a lay-and-then-back plan combined with a good stop loss. So always follow your advance lay/back plans with a strict stop loss as this is the way to succeed in the long run.

For example, if a team batting first in a Twenty20 match has a flying start and the odds are around 1.40 in the fourth over. As per the plan, we lay that team for £200 at 1.44. Now the back plan is very important. Suppose after the first wicket falls the odds reached around 1.60, then it is sensible to back 120% (or £240) at 1.62 because in Twenty20 wickets are of less importance than in any other format of the game.

For this trade it is very important that you place your back trade of £240 at 1.62 in advance because the odds can change within seconds to 1.50 (and sometimes without a ball being bowled).

You can then try and repeat this trade again.

It is also very important that you set a stop loss. I would set it at around 10 ticks at the most, as some of these matches can be extremely one-sided and a batting side's odds can shorten to between 1.01 – 1.10 within a few overs.

So, in summary, the back plan may be to back 80% at above 20-25 ticks (take early profit) or back 120% at above 20-25 ticks and try to repeat the trade during the match.

General tips

The following is a list of general things you should look for during a match.

1. If you are looking to lay the bowling team between 1.20 – 1.30, take time to consider who is coming to the crease next and whether any big hitting batsman remain or not.

2. Spin bowling around the 10-15 over period of the match is crucial in both innings. So teams that have good spinners are backable at this time.

3. A team chasing 60 runs in six overs look to have a big task, but 40 runs in three overs doesn't look as big, especially if there are wickets in hand. So you can consider laying the bowling team at around 1.10 – 1.20 in this situation.

4. A batting team whose odds are between 1.01 – 1.20 when chasing a good total represents a very good trading opportunity, especially after three wickets have fallen and 90+ runs required at 8+ runs per over. It is not easy to score at this run rate in any format of the game, and these teams should certainly not be priced between 1.10 – 1.20.

5. Looking through the previous games, the main rule would be to wait for any team to hit around 1.30 before laying them. So far this seems to be the best policy in Twenty20.

What to avoid in Twenty20 trading

Always avoid these situations as they will often lead to a loss:

1. Never back short odds (1.01 to 1.30) at any time of the match.

2. Don't allow a losing trade to get out of control and always employ a stop loss.

3. Avoid overtrading and overstaking.

4. Don't chase losses.

Bet Angel

Finally, a note on using software such as Bet Angel to trade the cricket.

With this software you can set a stop loss and even a trailing stop loss. Now this can be very useful, as a number of Twenty20 matches can be one-sided and dominated by the team batting first, and the odds always seem to go straight down.

For example, a favourite may win the toss and start the match at 1.70, only for the price to go down to 1.30 after a few overs. This happens very regularly and software such as Bet Angel can easily be employed by setting a stop loss or trailing stop loss, and following the batting side's price down in the first innings.

Looking at the data from the first two Indian Premier League Twenty20 tournaments I would look to back the favourite batting first anywhere between 1.7 to 1.8, and wait for the price to go down to 1.3 – 1.4. I would also set the stop loss at 2.00.

26. Golf

Golf lends itself well to the betting exchanges. A leaderboard can change many times during an event, and as there are four rounds there are plenty of opportunities to assess and change your positions.

It is also the fairest of all sports for both player and trader. Thrown matches, horses ridden to lose and additional factors that have to be taken into account in other sports are simply not present in golf trading. How many golfers do you know who would allow themselves to lose! In the PGA golf tournaments rankings, earnings and a desire to keep their tour card far outweigh any benefits to be had from throwing matches.

I really enjoy trading golf and love doing my homework on the event. It is certainly a sport where it helps to have an analytical brain and be very organised. Before putting any money down I keep a separate golfing diary for trading the PGA events. In the diary I keep a record of things such as stroke index, which holes are the hardest/easiest and the average number of strokes per hole. I also make a note of who is playing each hole. I am always using this information-gathering to assess the best trading options.

Information gathering and live feeds

Unfortunately, following both European and US live golf is not cheap. Sky TV cover the European tour and the satellite TV company Eurosport now have the rights to the US PGA golf. Also, thanks to the multiple adverts on the American TV companies, what you are watching is not live half of the time, so the only real alternative is to follow the tournaments on the PGA tour website. The website contains all the statistics you are likely to need before trading a tournament.

Your second and third trade

Laying is by far the best way of playing these markets, since providing you work out your strategy and know your maximum loss beforehand, a golfer's ride to victory is never straightforward – as the following example shows.

Example: South African tournament

Table 5.8: Laying Ernie Els for 5.5 at start of South African tournament

	Stake	Tot. Stake	Odds	Avg Odds	Liability	Tot. Liability
LAY	£30	£30	5.5	5.5	£135	
	£60	£90	3.5	4.16	£150	£285
	£150	£240	2.5	3.12	£225	£510
	£150	£390	2	2.69	£150	£660
BACK		£580	1.8			
	Lose £190 if wins. Lose £196 if finishes 2nd or worse					

In the above example at the start of the South African Open I decided to lay Ernie Els for 5.5 at the start of the tournament, hoping he was going to make a bad start.

1. My first bet was a £30 lay at odds of 5.5, which left me with a liability of £135. Unfortunately he made a good start and his odds went down to 3.5.

2. I then layed again for £60 at 3.5, which effectively meant I had layed £90 at average odds of 4.16. He continued to play well the next morning and his price went further down to 2.5.

3. Again I layed £150 at 2.5, which meant I had layed £240 at average odds of 3.12.

I then planned to lay Els again if his price went down to 2.0, and my stop loss was going to be 1.80; where, if this was hit, I would trade out for around a £196 loss.

As it happened, the round went on and Els dropped a couple of strokes while others picked up shots. This meant Els' odds drifted to 5.2, which was over the 3.12 average price I had layed. So I then did the following: backed Els at 5.2 for £240, which meant if Els went on to win I would win £498 and lose nothing if any of the other competitors went on to win. As golf is relatively unpredictable, I greened up, which meant I would win £95 whoever won.

Incidentally, Els went on to win the tournament, but as you can see from this example the odds change very dramatically and in golf it is very rare for a golfer to go three rounds without some problems along the way – as was the case with Ernie Els.

And using the above example I knew that whatever the outcome my maximum loss was limited to £196. Providing you stick to the rules (be disciplined and ensure you green up at the nearest available opportunity) golf can be extremely profitable when you are always looking two or three bets ahead.

Some stats to bear in mind

The best time to trade in a golf tournament is after the second round, when the tournament has settled down and the lower odds are available to lay.

The following facts should be taken into account before deciding which player you should lay.

Around 35% of leaders after the second round go on to win the tournament and 72% of the winners come from the top five. With this in mind you should use the following rules:

1. Consider only the top five on the leaderboard.

2. Looking at the top five, see those whose third round scoring average is better than their first two rounds' average. This is where the pressure starts, and you need to identify those who are likely to falter.

3. Consider only those players who are also in the top five par 4 scoring average over the first two rounds. This gives a good indication of how well the players are playing the primary holes and again highlights those who are likely to falter.

Low scoring tournaments

Many of the US PGA tournaments are regarded as drive and pitch events where the winning score often reaches 20 under. There are excellent opportunities to trade the early leaders of these tournaments with very little risk.

If a top 10 player hits the front and is leading in the clubhouse on the morning of the second round, you will often find that this player is trading at a very low price. Yet there may be up to 20 or more players yet to go out and play their rounds, and if the course is low-scoring you would hope that at least four or five of them will score low enough to come into contention or even take the lead.

Given this situation you are looking to lay the leader as soon as his round is complete.

The beauty of this strategy is that on a low scoring course half of the players are still to play, and if he is near the top he will not appear on the course again for over 24 hours.

Unless everyone else has a horrific round, the price of the player you have layed should not go down, and in my experience the price on offer for these early leaders is very distorted from their real chance of winning.

The other benefit is that whilst he is not on the course he cannot influence or improve further his own position. I would not promise that his price would drift dramatically, but the probability is it will drift enough to make a nice profit, and by the time he tees of for his third round your profit should be secure.

Players' reputations

On the other hand I am never afraid of players' reputations (unless of course it is the brilliant Tiger Woods). It always amazes me that after the first round of a tournament the likes of Vijay Singh, Ernie Els and Phil Mickelson can be lying in 40th place and eight strokes back but still be trading around the 5-8 mark.

These players are priced on reputation alone. I would always look to lay these players at the end of the first round, given the above circumstances. In my opinion there is just no way these players would win 20 times out of a hundred given these circumstances, and yet these are the odds that are on offer.

Hole-by-hole comparisons

After the first round is completed I always like to take a look at how each hole played, mentally making a note of the hardest and easiest. This is always useful, especially when there are a group of three or four holes where many shots have either been dropped or picked up.

As an example, I recently traded the Alfred Dunhill Championship in South Africa during the second round. Charles Schwartzel was the leader in the clubhouse at eight-under. Ernie Els was yet to start his round and was eight shots behind at level par and was trading at 8.

I could see that the afternoon starters were not having the best time of things and noted that there was a particularly difficult section between holes 7 and 12 – which included four of the hardest-rated holes with an average of two dropped shots during this period.

I was planning on laying Els but was waiting until he reached the 7th; during the first six holes he had picked up 3 shots, was 5 behind and was trading at 4 on approaching the 7th tee. This is where I placed my lay bet.

I figured that even if he got through the next six holes without dropping a stroke, he was still five behind and would not trade much lower. Unbelievably during this six-hole spell, he dropped five shots leaving him ten behind.

Of course, the reverse can also happen; a player in contention could be facing a group of holes where many strokes have been picked up. This would of course be a good opportunity to back this player, hoping he will pick up a couple of shots so that his odds will drop and you can collect a nice profit.

Final round trading

Trading against the leader in the final round of a tournament can be extremely profitable, as a dropped shot can mean a huge fluctuation in a player's odds.

If a leader or top player drops a shot in the first two rounds of an event, his and the general market price will hardly move. So when the back nine of the final day starts and the pressure intensifies for those in contention, this is an ideal time to get involved in these markets.

This is where my notes and trading diary play a huge part.

For example, Sergio García is leading Vijay Singh by one shot in the final round of a PGA event. Below are listed my thoughts for trading this event.

1. García is approaching the par 4, 14th which is proving the hardest hole on the course, averaging a score of 4.54, Sergio has also bogeyed this hole on two of the last three days.

2. I would then look at the stroke index and current position of his nearest rivals.

3. García is leading by a shot and he is on the hardest hole; his second place rival Vijay Singh is about to tee off on the par 5, 16th.

4. The 16th is yielding an average score of 4.6 and is regarded as the easiest hole on the course, and Vijay has birdied the hole on every single day.

5. There is a good possibility that there could be up to a two shot swing, which would alter García's price dramatically.

6. I would then look to lay García the moment he walks on to the 14th tee.

Now, obviously, the above scenario does not work out every time, but you are playing the percentage game and giving yourself an excellent chance of profiting.

A final note on golf

Never be afraid to oppose a player who is four shots clear, and is odds-on to win going into the final round. It is incredible the frequency with which odds on favourites get turned over, or at least present profitable trading opportunities.

Also, once you have gained a profit and your player is priced at around 1.05 – 1.10, always ensure that you green up at this stage. Again, you would be surprised at how many times players who trade at these odds with a few holes to play then go on to lose.

For the sake of a small percentage, always ensure that you green up for a guaranteed profit.

PART SIX

The Rules for Mastering Betfair

By way of summarising the major points made in this book, below are listed the 18 key rules for mastering Betfair.

Rule 1: Experience as many markets as possible

When opening an account and starting on Betfair, expose yourself to as many markets as possible to see which sports you are interested in that suit your individual trading style.

Rule 2: Always set yourself attainable goals

Set yourself a realistic time frame to learn the Betfair markets and to become competent. Also set yourself realistic financial goals that are proportionate to your bank.

Rule 3: Only trade with money you can afford to lose

Never play with previously allocated or borrowed money, and only trade with money you can afford to lose. You should only commit the amount of money that you are comfortable with; this will allow you to perform to the best of your abilities.

Rule 4: When testing a system, trade with minimum stakes

When testing a new trading system, test the system with the minimum stakes before committing large sums of your trading capital.

Rule 5: Always learn from your mistakes

On making a mistake, do not beat yourself up over it. Stop and think about what went wrong and, more importantly, how you can prevent the same thing from happening again in the future.

Rule 6: Keep a trading diary and review it everyday

Keep a trading diary that records all of your trades and review it every day. I believe that just having the discipline to follow this one rule could improve your trading dramatically.

Rule 7: Devise a trading plan

Once you are happy using the Betfair site and are happy with the markets that you will be trading, take the necessary time to construct a trading plan.

Rule 8: Always trade using a system

You must always remember that it is not about the profitability of individual trades but the consistent results of weeks and months of trading your system that will ultimately prove profitable.

Rule 9: Learn how the markets react

Spend a year watching how the markets behave and build a plan around your findings.

Rule 10: Spend time back-testing your system

The best way of forming a true opinion of whether a trading system will be profitable or not is by back-testing to see how the system performed in the past. Ensure that you test at least 100 and preferably 300 data points.

Rule 11: Ensure your strategy has historic profitability

Always ensure that your system has a solid history of profitability, and that on looking back in the past your winning trades have outperformed your losing trades.

Rule 12: Only trade high probability trades

A high probability trade has a proven historic record of working and generally the financial risk is low compared to the amount that can be made. When executing this trade you should be able to explain to someone in plain English the logic of what you are doing, the risk involved, and the level of profit you are aiming to achieve.

Rule 13: Protect your bank

To protect your bank, and before entering any trade, you should always assess the risk first and know beforehand when you are going to get out of the trade.

Rule 14: Risk only 1–2% of your bank on any one trade

Always ensure you follow the five points of the Money Management Plan and never risk more than 2% of your bank on any one trade.

1. Identify your market
2. Pre-define your entry and exit positions
3. Identify where your stop loss is going to be placed
4. Calculate your position size using the 1-2% rule
5. Execute the trade

Rule 15: Accept fully that you may lose the amount risked on each trade

You are not going to win on every trade and you have to accept that some of your trades are going to be losers. Accept this and discipline yourself to stick with your pre-planned system.

Rule 16: Take a contrarian view

Never blindly follow the money and back low-priced favourites. There are many excellent low-risk trades available if you take the time and think outside the box.

Rule 17: Trade within your individual time frame

Experiment in the markets and find the sports that are consistent with your natural time frame.

Rule 18: Always keep your trading in perspective

Keep your trading in perspective and find your own balance in life, and realise that there is more to life than just trading the sporting markets.

Conclusion

I hope that you have found this book useful, whether you are completely new to the Betfair markets or are an experienced trader. If you have a financial background I hope that you have now seen the great potential that these sporting markets offer.

After you have read through the various sections and have found a sport and a system that you are happy trading, now is the time to actually take the risk and place the trade. Many new traders hesitate at this point – because they are now about to risk their hard-earned money, rather than just think about it.

It is at this moment that you may feel pangs of fear!

This is only natural and happens to most traders. But so long as you are fully aware that from time to time you will have losing days, and you always ensure that your losses are kept to a pre-determined amount, you should be all right, and end up profitable over the long-term.

 Remember: never let your losses run, and always place a stop loss.

Finally, many thanks for taking the time to read this book. I wish you all the best and good luck with your trading!

APPENDICES

I. A Month Trading Tennis

The following pages show the results of trading the Madrid and Warsaw Open Tennis tournaments between 9-23 May 2009 using the rules set out below. This is shown so that you can have confidence in the system; it also highlights the patience, discipline and time required to trade these markets profitably.

The Rules

1. If the SP (starting price) is between 1.90 – 1.21, lay as soon as price hits 1.25; providing this is done during the first set of the match. Preferably you should be laying when the price just goes straight down to the 1.25 level from the SP.

2. If the price goes further down to 1.13, double your lay then back at 2.00 and green up.

3. Set a stop loss after the price has risen above the SP at 1.10.

4. If the price goes up 10 ticks from the SP before coming down to the 1.25 level then there is no bet.

Madrid Open

1st Round

BET 1: SP 1.50 NO BET PRICE DID NOT TOUCH 1.25 IN 1st SET +£0.00
TOTAL +£00.00

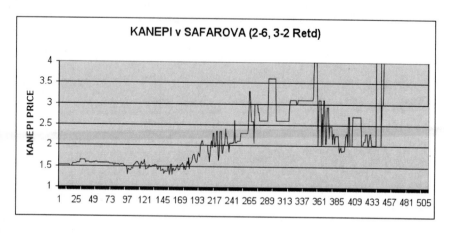

KANEPI v SAFAROVA (2-6, 3-2 Retd)

BET 2: SP 1.68 LAY £100 AT 1.25: LAY £200 AT 1.13: LOST -£51.00
TOTAL -£51.00

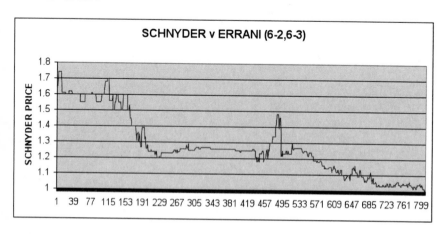

SCHNYDER v ERRANI (6-2,6-3)

BET 3: SP 1.30 NO BET PRICE DID NOT TOUCH 1.25 IN 1st SET +£0.00
TOTAL -£51.00

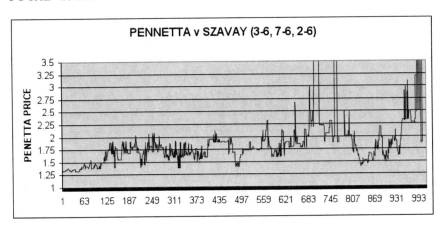

BET 4: SP 1.28 NO BET PRICE DID NOT TOUCH 1.25 IN 1st SET +£0.00
TOTAL -£51.00

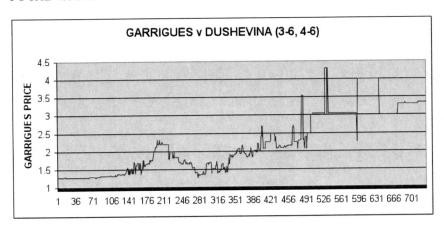

BET 5: SP 1.31 NO BET PRICE WENT 10 TICKS ABOVE SP BEFORE
HITTING 1.25 +£0.00; TOTAL – £51.00

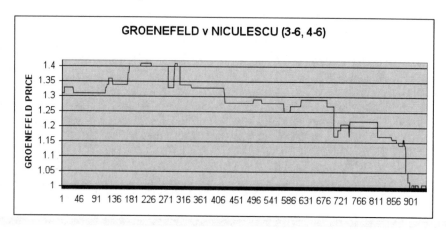

BET 6: SP 1.70 LAY £100 AT 1.25 THEN LAY £200 AT 1.13; GREEN UP
AT 2.00 +£118.27 TOTAL +£67.27

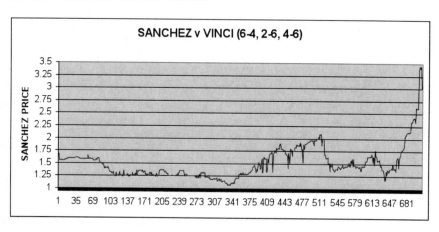

BET 7: SP 1.40 NO BET PRICE DID NOT TOUCH 1.25 IN 1st SET +£0.00
TOTAL +£67.27

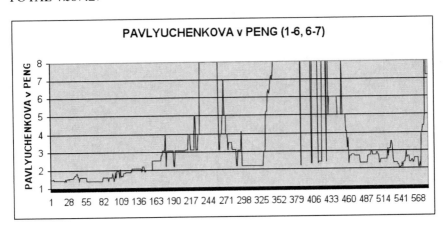

BET 8: SP 1.55 NO BET PRICE WENT 10 TICKS ABOVE SP BEFORE
HITTING 1.25 +£0.00; TOTAL +£67.27

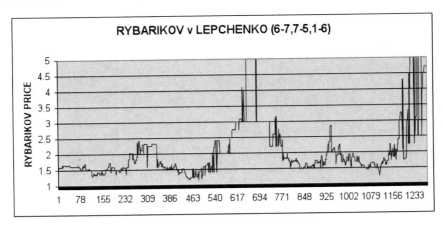

BET 9: SP 1.70 NO BET PRICE DID NOT TOUCH 1.25 IN 1st SET +£0.00
TOTAL +£67.27

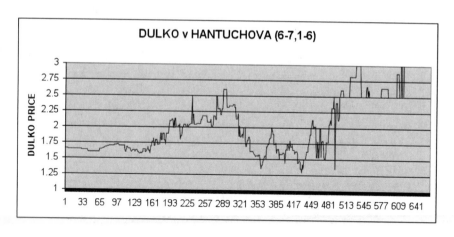

2nd Round

BET 10: SP 1.55 NO BET PRICE WENT 10 TICKS ABOVE SP BEFORE
HITTING 1.25 +£0.00; TOTAL +£67.27

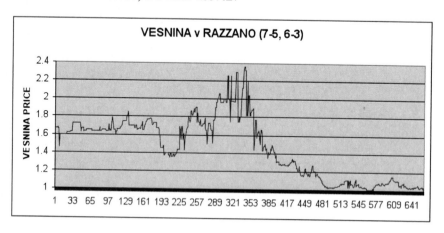

BET 11: SP 1.70 NO BET PRICE WENT 10 TICKS ABOVE SP BEFORE HITTING 1.25 +£0.00; TOTAL +£67.27

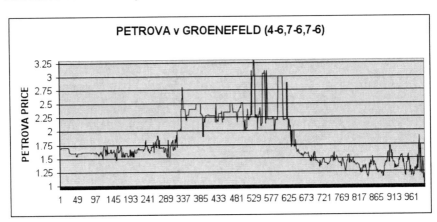

BET 12: SP 1.75 NO BET PRICE WENT 10 TICKS ABOVE SP BEFORE HITTING 1.25 +£0.00; TOTAL +£67.27

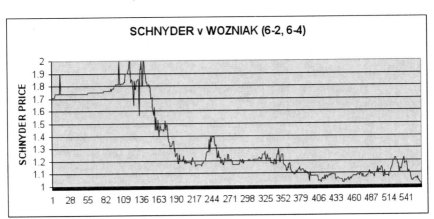

BET 13: SP 1.90 NO BET PRICE WENT 10 TICKS ABOVE SP BEFORE
HITTING 1.25 +£0.00; TOTAL +£67.27

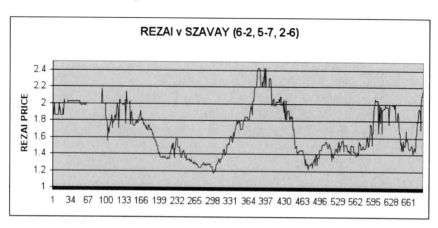

BET 14: SP 1.29 LAY £100 AT 1.25; LAY £200 AT 1.13 AND WENT 10
POINTS ABOVE SP BEFORE COMING BACK DOWN STOP LOSS AT
1.10; -£21.00 TOTAL +£46.27

BET 15: SP 1.90 NO BET PRICE DID NOT TOUCH 1.25 IN 1st SET +£0.00 TOTAL +£46.27

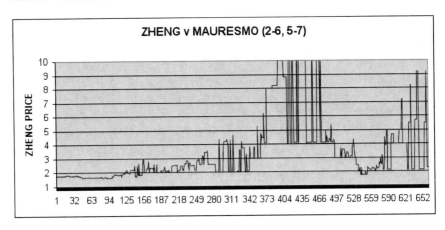

BET 16: SP 1.60 NO BET PRICE DID NOT TOUCH 1.25 IN 1st SET +£0.00 TOTAL +£46.27

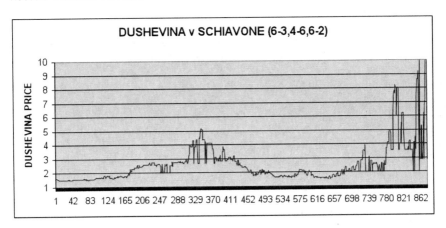

BET 17: SP 1.80 NO BET PRICE DID NOT TOUCH 1.25 IN 1st SET +£0.00 TOTAL +£46.27

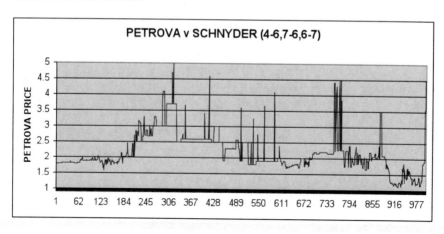

BET 18: SP 1.41 LAY £100 AT 1.25 AND WENT 10 POINTS ABOVE SP BEFORE COMING BACK DOWN STOP LOSS AT SP; GREEN UP +£10.78 TOTAL +£57.05

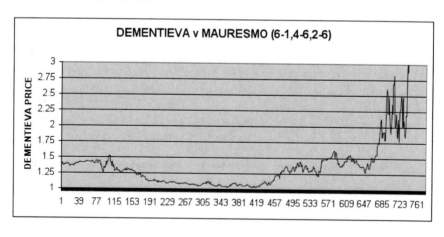

BET 19: SP 1.90 NO LAY £100 AT 1.25; GREEN UP AT 2.00 +£35.62; TOTAL +£92.67

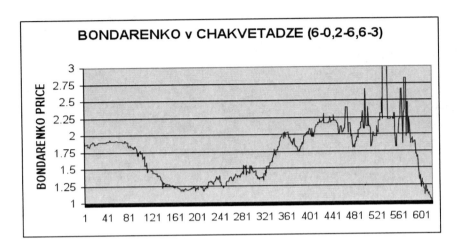

BET 20 SP 1.20 LAY £100 AT 1.20; AND WENT 10 POINTS ABOVE SP BEFORE COMING BACK DOWN STOP LOSS AT SP; +£0.00 TOTAL +£92.67

BET 21: SP 1.22 LAY £100 AT 1.22 THEN LAY £200 AT 1.13; GREEN UP
AT 2.00 +£119.70 TOTAL +£212.37

BET 22: SP 1.46 LAY £100 AT 1.25: LAY £200 AT 1.13: LOST -£51.00
TOTAL +£161.37

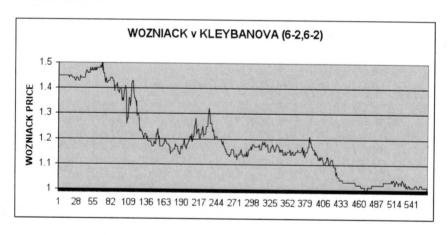

Final

BET 23: SP 1.37 LAY £100 AT 1.25: LAY £200 AT 1.13: LOST -£51.00
TOTAL +£110.37

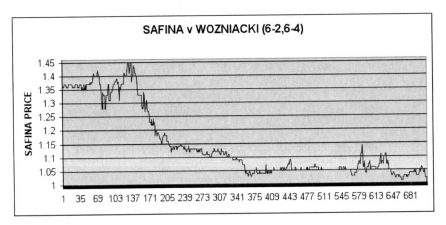

Warsaw Open

1st Round

BET 24: SP 1.32 LAY £100 AT 1.25 THEN LAY £200 AT 1.13; GREEN UP
AT 2.00 +£118.27 TOTAL +£228.64

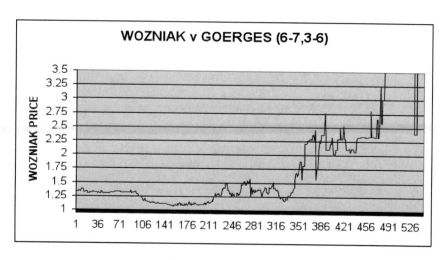

BET 25: SP 1.40 LAY £100 AT 1.25 THEN LAY £200 AT 1.13; GREEN UP
AT 2.00 +£118.27 TOTAL +£346.91

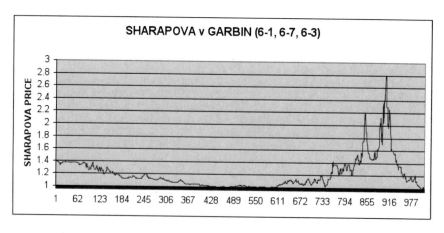

BET 26: SP 1.23 LAY £100 AT 1.23 THEN LAY £200 AT 1.13; GREEN UP
AT 2.00 +£119.22 TOTAL +£466.13

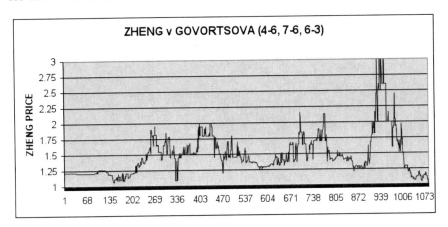

BET 27: SP 1.78 NO BET PRICE WENT 10 TICKS ABOVE SP BEFORE
HITTING 1.25 +£0.00; TOTAL +£466.13

BET 28: SP 1.45 LAY £100 AT 1.25: LAY £200 AT 1.13: LOST -£51.00 TOTAL +£415.13

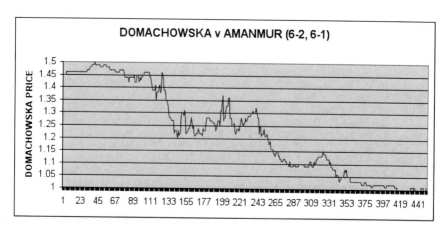

BET 29: SP 1.75 LAY £100 AT 1.25 THEN LAY £200 AT 1.13; GREEN UP AT 2.00 +£118.27 TOTAL +£533.40

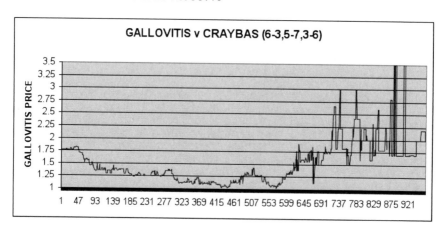

BET 30: SP 1.25 LAY £100 AT 1.25; GREEN UP AT 2.00 +£35.62 TOTAL +£569.02

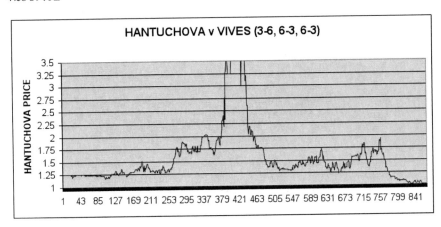

BET 31: SP 1.68 NO BET PRICE WENT 10 TICKS ABOVE SP BEFORE HITTING 1.25 +£0.00; TOTAL +£569.02

BET 32: SP 1.80 NO BET PRICE DID NOT TOUCH 1.25 IN 1st SET +£0.00 TOTAL +£569.02

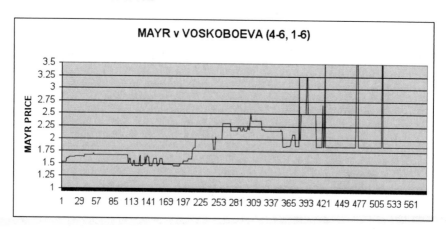

BET 33: SP 1.80 NO BET PRICE DID NOT TOUCH 1.25 IN 1st SET +£0.00 TOTAL +£569.02

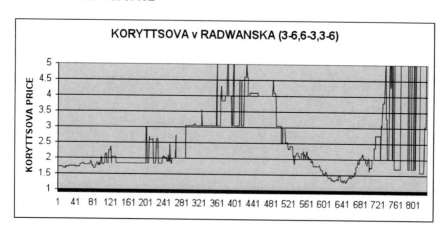

2nd Round

BET 34: SP 1.32 LAY £100 AT 1.25; AND WENT 10 POINTS ABOVE SP BEFORE COMING BACK DOWN STOP LOSS AT SP; +£0.00 TOTAL +£569.02

BET 35: SP 1.45 NO BET PRICE DID NOT TOUCH 1.25 IN 1st SET +£0.00 TOTAL +£569.02

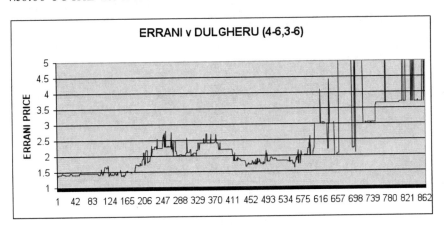

BET 36: SP 1.75 NO BET PRICE DID NOT TOUCH 1.25 IN 1st SET +£0.00 TOTAL +£569.02

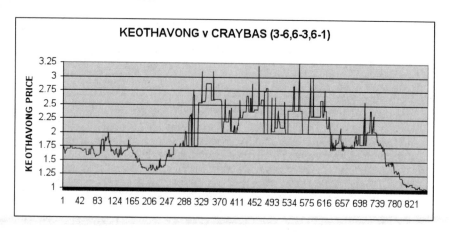

BET 37: SP 1.40 NO BET PRICE DID NOT TOUCH 1.25 IN 1st SET +£0.00 TOTAL +£569.02

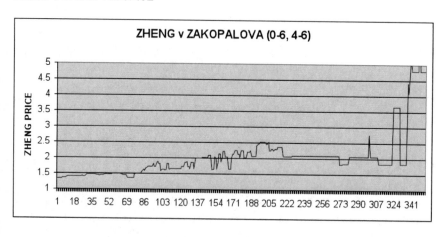

BET 38: SP 1.27 LAY £100 AT 1.25; AND WENT 10 POINTS ABOVE SP BEFORE COMING BACK DOWN STOP LOSS AT SP; +£0.00 TOTAL +£569.02

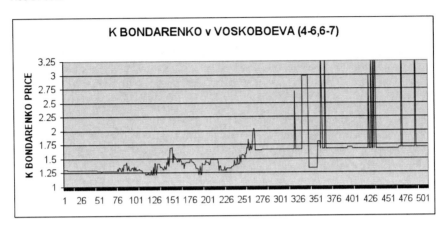

BET 39: SP 1.32 NO BET PRICE DID NOT TOUCH 1.25 IN 1ˢᵗ SET +£0.00 TOTAL +£569.02

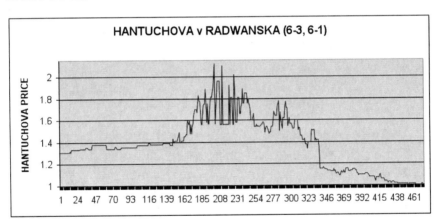

BET 40: SP 1.65 NO BET PRICE DID NOT TOUCH 1.25 IN 1st SET +£0.00 TOTAL +£569.02

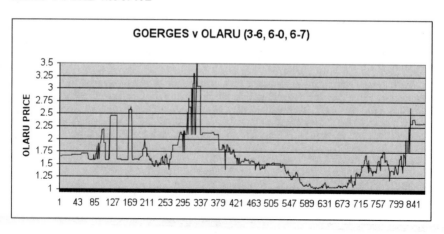

Quarter-finals

BET 41: SP 1.95 LAY £100 AT 1.25: LAY £200 AT 1.13: LOST -£51.00 TOTAL +£518.02

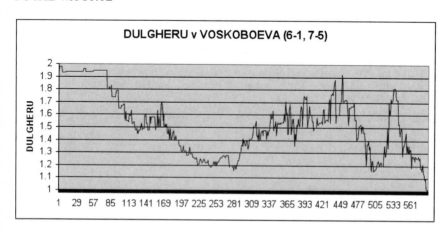

BET 42: SP 1.70 NO BET PRICE DID NOT TOUCH 1.25 IN 1st SET +£0.00 TOTAL +£518.02

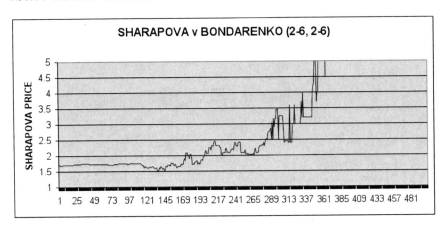

BET 43: SP 1.85 NO BET PRICE WENT 10 TICKS ABOVE SP BEFORE HITTING 1.25 +£0.00; TOTAL +£518.02

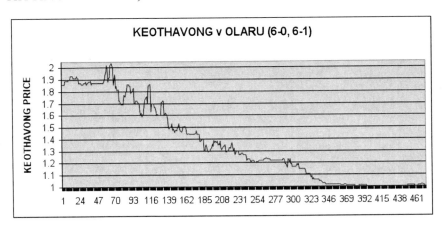

BET 44: SP 1.43 LAY £100 AT 1.25; LAY £200 AT 1.13 AND WENT 10
POINTS ABOVE SP BEFORE COMING BACK DOWN STOP LOSS AT
1.10; -£21.00 TOTAL +£497.02

Semi-final

BET 45: SP 1.95 LAY £100 AT 1.25; GREEN UP AT 2.00 +£35.62 TOTAL
+£532.64

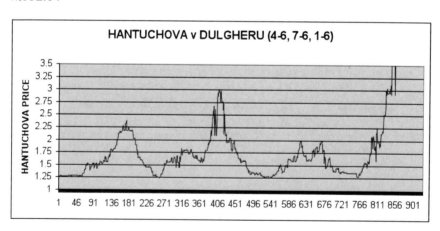

BET 46: SP 1.23 LAY £100 AT 1.23 THEN PRICE WENT 10 TICKS ABOVE SP STOP LOSS AT SP +£0.00; TOTAL +£532.64

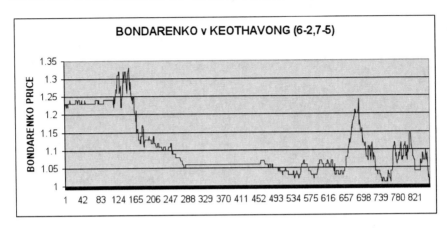

Final

BET 47: SP 1.23 LAY £100 AT 1.23 THEN PRICE WENT 10 TICKS ABOVE SP STOP LOSS AT SP +£0.00; TOTAL +£532.64

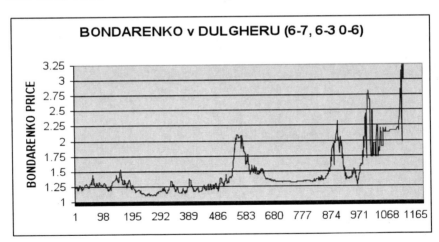

II. Results of Analysis on Tennis Strategies

Introduction

In the following you will see two sets of data taken from spreadsheets that highlight the two tennis strategies explained earlier in the book.

The data has been taken from both men's and women's three set matches.

- The first 111 lines highlight those matches where the price on the favourite did not hit the low of 1.25.

- The next lines (1-265) indicate all of the matches where the price at some stage traded above the starting price after hitting 1.25. Those lines that are shaded indicate winning trades where the price moved up to 2.00 and 1.50 respectively.

- Lines 266-305 highlight all of those matches where the price hit 1.25 but the player did not trade above the starting price.

[If you would like a copy of the Excel spreadsheet please email me at masteringbetfair@petenordsted.com.]

Back at 2.00 strategy

Here is an explanation to each column –

- **Column A** is the starting price or available lay price of the favourite prior to going in-play.

- **Column B** is the low price it hit before rising.

- **Column C** is the highest price the selection hit.

- **Column D** highlights whether the favourite won or lost.

- **Column E** shows the losing trades and how much would have been lost on each trade.

- **Column F** shows what happens to the losing trades and how much would have been lost on each trade after employing the stop loss rule.

- **Column G** shows those trades that hit 2.00 and you then went on to green up at 2.00. It also highlights the amount that would have been won on that trade.

- **Column H** shows those trades that hit 1.50 and a straight back bet was then placed. It also highlights the amount that would have been won on that trade.

	A	B	C	D	E	F	G	H
	PRICE	LOW	HIGH	WON /LOST	LOSERS	STOP LOSS 1.10	Green Up @2.00	BACK @ 2.00
1	1.50	1.50	1.57	Won				
2	1.49	1.46	1000.00	Lost				
3	1.48	1.45	1000.00	Lost				
4	1.48	1.45	1.65	Won				
5	1.45	1.45	1.55	Won				
6	1.50	1.45	5.30	Won				
7	1.46	1.44	1000.00	Lost				
8	1.44	1.44	32.00	Lost				
9	1.50	1.44	1.80	Won				
10	1.50	1.43	1000.00	Won				
11	1.47	1.43	1.55	Won				
12	1.45	1.43	1.47	Won				
13	1.50	1.42	2.02	Won				
14	1.43	1.42	1.57	Won				
15	1.50	1.42	1.61	Won				
16	1.50	1.42	1000.00	Lost				
17	1.41	1.41	1.42	Won				
18	1.43	1.41	1.77	Won				
19	1.49	1.40	1.54	Won				
20	1.45	1.40	1.62	Won				
21	1.40	1.40	1.55	Won				
22	1.44	1.40	1.55	Won				
23	1.44	1.40	1.58	Won				
24	1.42	1.39	1.65	Won				
25	1.46	1.39	1.50	Won				
26	1.44	1.38	1.95	Won				
27	1.42	1.38	1000.00	Lost				
28	1.39	1.38	1.42	Won				
29	1.41	1.38	1.60	Won				
30	1.39	1.38	1.55	Won				
31	1.40	1.37	1.51	Won				
32	1.45	1.37	1.49	Won				
33	1.50	1.36	1000.00	Lost				
34	1.47	1.36	3.50	Won				
35	1.41	1.36	12.00	Lost				
36	1.41	1.36	4.20	Won				
37	1.38	1.36	1.46	Won				
38	1.46	1.36	1.69	Won				
39	1.39	1.36	1.70	Won				
40	1.49	1.36	2.06	Won				
41	1.46	1.36	1000.00	Lost				
42	1.49	1.35	100.00	Lost				
43	1.48	1.35	1.54	Won				
44	1.44	1.35	2.20	Won				
45	1.42	1.35	2.26	Won				
46	1.42	1.35	1.46	Won				
47	1.38	1.35	1000.00	Lost				
48	1.35	1.35	1.37	Won				
49	1.50	1.35	100.00	Lost				

50	1.44	1.35	1000.00	Lost					
51	1.41	1.35	2.22	Won					
52	1.40	1.34	1.52	Won					
53	1.38	1.34	65.00	Lost					
54	1.38	1.34	1000.00	Lost					
55	1.44	1.33	40.00	Lost					
56	1.42	1.33	1.61	Won					
57	1.37	1.33	2.62	Won					
58	1.36	1.33	1.40	Won					
59	1.34	1.33	1.43	Won					
60	1.38	1.33	1.48	Won					
61	1.34	1.32	4.00	Won					
62	1.50	1.32	1000.00	Lost					
63	1.41	1.32	2.08	Won					
64	1.39	1.32	1.87	Won					
65	1.37	1.32	2.00	Won					
66	1.34	1.32	1000.00	Lost					
67	1.34	1.32	1.48	Won					
68	1.40	1.32	1.56	Won					
69	1.36	1.32	1.79	Won					
70	1.50	1.31	5.10	Won					
71	1.37	1.31	1000.00	Lost					
72	1.40	1.31	1000.00	Lost					
73	1.40	1.30	1.69	Won					
74	1.39	1.30	1.74	Won					
75	1.39	1.30	1.72	Won					
76	1.39	1.30	1.60	Won					
77	1.37	1.30	1.50	Won					
78	1.36	1.30	1.74	Won					
79	1.32	1.30	1.50	Won					
80	1.30	1.30	55.00	Lost					
81	1.34	1.30	1000.00	Lost					
82	1.42	1.30	1.43	Won					
83	1.35	1.30	1000.00	Lost					
84	1.37	1.30	1.40	Won					
85	1.50	1.29	1000.00	Lost					
86	1.48	1.29	2.84	Won					
87	1.39	1.29	3.40	Won					
88	1.31	1.29	1.70	Won					
89	1.44	1.29	1000.00	Won					
90	1.36	1.29	1000.00	Lost					
91	1.46	1.28	200.00	Lost					
92	1.31	1.28	5.50	Won					
93	1.31	1.28	1.36	Won					
94	1.48	1.28	1.59	Won					
95	1.39	1.28	1.43	Won					
96	1.38	1.28	6.80	Won					
97	1.42	1.27	25.00	Lost					
98	1.38	1.27	1.72	Won					
99	1.30	1.27	1.34	Won					
100	1.35	1.27	1.42	Won					
101	1.31	1.27	1.55	Won					
102	1.34	1.27	6.60	Won					
103	1.35	1.27	2.80	Won					
104	1.32	1.27	1.80	Won					
105	1.38	1.26	1.56	Won					

106	1.27	1.26	1.30	Won				
107	1.47	1.26	3.70	Won				
108	1.45	1.26	20.00	Won				
109	1.43	1.26	1.74	Won				
110	1.37	1.26	1.43	Won				
111	1.33	1.26	1.92	Won	LOSERS	STOP LOSS 1.10	Green Up @2	BACK @ 2.00

1	1.38	1.25	400.00	Lost			37.5	
2	1.46	1.25	2.68	Won			37.5	75
3	1.30	1.25	1.76	Won	-25	-15		
4	1.41	1.25	1.69	Won	-25	-15		
5	1.30	1.25	1.34	Won	-25	-15		
6	1.26	1.25	1.27	Won	-25	-15		
7	1.38	1.25	500.00	Lost			37.5	
8	1.30	1.25	55.00	Lost			37.5	
9	1.46	1.25	4.60	Won			37.5	75
10	1.50	1.25	1.59	Won	-25	-15		
11	1.35	1.25	1.82	Won	-25	-15		
12	1.30	1.25	150.00	Lost			37.5	
13	1.29	1.25	3.70	Won			37.5	75
14	1.29	1.25	1.36	Won	-25	-15		
15	1.26	1.24	5.00	Won			37.5	75
16	1.39	1.24	1.70	Won	-25	-15		
17	1.43	1.24	1.50	Won	-25	-15		
18	1.27	1.24	1.38	Won	-25	-15		
19	1.26	1.24	1.35	Won	-25	-15		
20	1.24	1.24	1.32	Won	-24	-14		
21	1.33	1.24	1000.00	Lost			37.5	
22	1.46	1.23	3.15	Won			37.5	75
23	1.40	1.23	2.12	Won			37.5	75
24	1.33	1.23	1.62	Won	-25	-15		
25	1.33	1.23	1.50	Won	-25	-15		
26	1.29	1.23	1.43	Won	-25	-15		
27	1.29	1.23	1.34	Won	-25	-15		
28	1.24	1.23	1.28	Won	-24	-14		
29	1.39	1.23	6.00	Lost			37.5	
30	1.29	1.22	1000.00	Lost			37.5	
31	1.23	1.22	8.00	Won			38.5	77
32	1.38	1.22	2.44	Won			37.5	75
33	1.39	1.22	1.80	Won	-25	-15		
34	1.28	1.22	1.31	Won	-25	-15		
35	1.24	1.22	1.30	Won	-24	-14		
36	1.32	1.22	1000.00	Lost			37.5	
37	1.49	1.21	1000.00	Won			37.5	75
38	1.48	1.21	1000.00	Won			37.5	75
39	1.36	1.21	1000.00	Lost			37.5	
40	1.29	1.21	90.00	Lost			37.5	
41	1.29	1.21	2.32	Won			37.5	75
42	1.31	1.21	1.77	Won	-25	-15		
43	1.45	1.21	1.62	Won	-25	-15		

44	1.22	1.21	1.58	Won	-22	-12		
45	1.30	1.21	1.45	Won	-25	-15		
46	1.31	1.21	1.40	Won	-25	-15		
47	1.29	1.21	1.35	Won	-25	-15		
48	1.23	1.21	1.32	Won	-23	-13		
49	1.24	1.21	1.30	Won	-24	-14		
50	1.25	1.21	3.30	Won			37.5	75
51	1.33	1.21	110.00	Lost			37.5	
52	1.36	1.21	1000.00	Lost			37.5	
53	1.29	1.21	1.38	Won	-25	-15		
54	1.42	1.21	1.58	Won	-25	-15		
55	1.23	1.21	1.35	Won	-23	-13		
56	1.23	1.20	150.00	Won			38.5	77
57	1.42	1.20	80.00	Lost			37.5	
58	1.49	1.20	4.30	Won			37.5	75
59	1.36	1.20	3.00	Won			37.5	75
60	1.39	1.20	2.68	Won			37.5	75
61	1.36	1.20	2.02	Won			37.5	75
62	1.22	1.20	2.00	Won			39	78
63	1.24	1.20	1.95	Won	-24	-14		
64	1.22	1.20	1.89	Won	-22	-12		
65	1.29	1.20	1.46	Won	-25	-15		
66	1.24	1.20	1.43	Won	-24	-14		
67	1.38	1.20	1000.00	Lost			37.5	
68	1.28	1.20	1.59	Won	-25	-15		
69	1.21	1.20	1.68	Won	-21	-11		
70	1.45	1.20	2.22	Won	-25	-15		
71	1.45	1.20	1000.00	Lost			37.5	
72	1.38	1.20	1000.00	Lost			37.5	
73	1.30	1.20	1.42	Won	-25	-15		
74	1.23	1.20	1.24	Won	-23	-13		
75	1.23	1.19	1000.00	Lost			37.5	
76	1.23	1.19	250.00	Lost			37.5	
77	1.22	1.19	1.76	Won	-22	-12		
78	1.21	1.19	1.50	Won	-21	-11		
79	1.29	1.19	1.35	Won	-25	-15		
80	1.20	1.19	1.23	Won	-20	-10		
81	1.24	1.19	1.30	Won	-24	-14		
82	1.27	1.19	1.35	Won	-25	-15		
83	1.20	1.19	1.21	Won	-20	-10		
84	1.50	1.18	1000.00	Lost			37.5	
85	1.31	1.18	1000.00	Lost			37.5	
86	1.24	1.18	120.00	Lost			37.5	
87	1.30	1.18	1.59	Won	-25	-15		
88	1.29	1.18	1.45	Won	-25	-15		
89	1.21	1.18	1.22	Won	-21	-11		
90	1.20	1.18	1.24	Won	-20	-10		
91	1.31	1.17	26.00	Won			37.5	75
92	1.21	1.17	2.36	Won			39.5	79
93	1.38	1.17	2.20	Won			37.5	75
94	1.36	1.17	1.70	Won	-25	-15		
95	1.29	1.17	1.67	Won	-25	-15		
96	1.23	1.17	1.25	Won	-23	-13		
97	1.32	1.17	3.50	Won	-25	-15		
98	1.27	1.17	2.20	Won			37.5	75
99	1.21	1.17	1.31	Won	-21	-11		

100	1.29	1.16	1000.00	Lost			37.5	
101	1.21	1.16	2.22	Won			39.5	79
102	1.22	1.16	1.66	Won	-22	-12		
103	1.34	1.16	1.40	Won	-25	-15		
104	1.25	1.16	1.31	Won	-25	-15		
105	1.38	1.16	5.00	Won			37.5	75
106	1.31	1.16	2.08	Won			37.5	75
107	1.42	1.15	80.00	Lost			37.5	
108	1.21	1.15	50.00	Lost			37.5	
109	1.42	1.15	14.00	Lost			37.5	
110	1.38	1.15	4.30	Lost			37.5	
111	1.34	1.15	3.50	Won			37.5	75
112	1.21	1.15	3.25	Won			39.5	79
113	1.30	1.15	1.50	Won	-25	-15		
114	1.21	1.15	1.45	Won	-21	-11		
115	1.38	1.15	1.44	Won	-25	-15		
116	1.25	1.15	1.29	Won	-25	-15		
117	1.27	1.15	1.31	Won	-25	-15		
118	1.38	1.15	2.00	Won			37.5	75
119	1.37	1.15	4.00	Won			37.5	75
120	1.20	1.15	1.62	Won	-20	-10		
121	1.40	1.14	1000.00	Lost			37.5	
122	1.48	1.14	2.82	Won			37.5	75
123	1.39	1.14	1.79	Won	-25	-15		
124	1.49	1.14	1.76	Won	-25	-15		
125	1.34	1.14	2.62	Won			37.5	75
126	1.24	1.14	300.00	Lost			37.5	
127	1.20	1.14	1.68	Won	-20	-10		
128	1.39	1.13	200.00	Lost			124.5	
129	1.46	1.13	9.20	Lost			124.5	
130	1.48	1.13	2.78	Won			124.5	249
131	1.36	1.13	2.10	Won			124.5	249
132	1.33	1.13	1.75	Won	-51	-21		
133	1.39	1.13	1.55	Won	-51	-21		
134	1.21	1.13	1.29	Won	-47	-17		
135	1.50	1.13	120.00	Lost			124.5	
136	1.32	1.13	2.02	Won			124.5	249
137	1.40	1.12	1000.00	Lost			124.5	
138	1.40	1.12	1000.00	Lost			124.5	
139	1.30	1.12	55.00	Lost			125.5	
140	1.35	1.12	4.10	Won			124.5	249
141	1.39	1.12	2.50	Won			124.5	249
142	1.49	1.12	2.26	Won			124.5	249
143	1.23	1.12	2.12	Won			125.5	251
144	1.49	1.12	2.00	Won			124.5	249
145	1.46	1.12	1.65	Won	-51	-21		
146	1.44	1.12	1.52	Won	-51	-21		
147	1.33	1.12	1.46	Won	-51	-21		
148	1.23	1.12	1.26	Won	-49	-19		
149	1.44	1.12	2.44	Won			124.5	249
150	1.33	1.12	1.60	Won	-51	-21		
151	1.26	1.12	1.66	Won	-51	-21		
152	1.31	1.12	160.00	Lost	-51	-21		
153	1.40	1.12	1000.00	Lost			124.5	
154	1.20	1.12	1.23	Won	-46	-16		
155	1.31	1.11	1000.00	Lost			124.5	

156	1.22	1.11	1000.00	Lost				124.5	
157	1.22	1.11	100.00	Lost				124.5	
158	1.45	1.11	5.10	Won				124.5	249
159	1.26	1.11	2.50	Won				124.5	249
160	1.36	1.11	2.20	Won				124.5	249
161	1.45	1.11	2.00	Won				124.5	249
162	1.48	1.11	1.55	Won	-51	-21			
163	1.25	1.11	1.43	Won	-51	-21			
164	1.33	1.11	70.00	Lost				124.5	
165	1.30	1.11	1.51	Won	-51	-21			
166	1.36	1.11	90.00	Lost				124.5	
167	1.49	1.11	4.60	Won				124.5	249
168	1.27	1.11	1.73	Won	-51	-21			
169	1.21	1.11	1.53	Won	-47	-17			
170	1.48	1.10	15.00	Lost				124.5	
171	1.35	1.10	2.10	Won				124.5	249
172	1.49	1.10	2.00	Won				124.5	249
173	1.27	1.10	1.87	Won	-51	-21			
174	1.35	1.10	2.00	Won				124.5	249
175	1.30	1.10	1.37	Won	-51	-21			
176	1.45	1.10	1000.00	Lost				124.5	
177	1.30	1.10	1.65	Won	-51	-21			
178	1.24	1.10	1000.00	Lost				124.5	
179	1.41	1.09	1000.00	Lost				124.5	
180	1.41	1.09	1000.00	Lost				124.5	
181	1.34	1.09	32.00	Lost				124.5	
182	1.29	1.09	10.00	Won				124.5	249
183	1.34	1.09	5.00	Lost				124.5	
184	1.36	1.09	3.80	Won				124.5	249
185	1.20	1.09	2.36	Won				127	254
186	1.37	1.09	2.00	Won				124.5	249
187	1.36	1.09	1.81	Won	-51	-21			
188	1.36	1.09	1.76	Won	-51	-21			
189	1.23	1.09	1.60	Won	-49	-19			
190	1.25	1.09	1.30	Won	-51	-21			
191	1.23	1.09	1.26	Won	-51	-21			
192	1.34	1.09	21.00	Lost				124.5	
193	1.27	1.09	1.40	Won	-51	-21			
194	1.28	1.08	11.00	Lost				124.5	
195	1.33	1.08	1.75	Won	-51	-21			
196	1.24	1.08	1.44	Won	-50	-20			
197	1.33	1.08	1.35	Won	-51	-21			
198	1.29	1.08	1.50	Won	-51	-21			
199	1.21	1.08	6.00	Won				124.5	249
200	1.40	1.08	1.81	Won	-51	-21			
201	1.23	1.08	1.45	Won	-49	-19			
202	1.37	1.07	1000.00	Won				124.5	249
203	1.21	1.07	1000.00	Lost				124.5	
204	1.38	1.07	100.00	Lost				124.5	
205	1.43	1.07	5.00	Lost				124.5	
206	1.44	1.07	2.42	Won				124.5	249
207	1.22	1.07	1.41	Won	-48	-18			
208	1.23	1.07	1.35	Won	-49	-19			
209	1.21	1.07	1.30	Won	-46	-16			
210	1.34	1.07	1.44	Won	-51	-21			
211	1.27	1.07	1.30	Won	-51	-21			

212	1.28	1.06	1000.00	Lost			124.5	
213	1.39	1.06	2.08	Won			124.5	249
214	1.34	1.06	1.64	Won	-51	-21		
215	1.21	1.06	1.60	Won	-47	-17		
216	1.39	1.06	2.20	Won			124.5	249
217	1.28	1.06	4.80	Won			124.5	249
218	1.50	1.05	1000.00	Lost			124.5	
219	1.32	1.05	1000.00	Lost			124.5	
220	1.34	1.05	5.00	Lost			124.5	
221	1.36	1.05	3.65	Won			124.5	249
222	1.23	1.05	2.12	Won			125.5	251
223	1.35	1.05	2.08	Won			124.5	249
224	1.37	1.05	1.72	Won	-51	-21		
225	1.42	1.05	1.63	Won	-51	-21		
226	1.35	1.05	2.28	Won			124.5	249
227	1.28	1.05	2.80	Won			124.5	249
228	1.46	1.05	990.00	Lost			124.5	
229	1.31	1.05	2.20	Won			124.5	249
230	1.25	1.05	50.00	Lost			124.5	
231	1.25	1.05	2.72	Won			124.5	249
232	1.32	1.04	1000.00	Lost			124.5	
233	1.33	1.04	5.00	Lost			124.5	
234	1.27	1.04	5.00	Won			124.5	249
235	1.45	1.04	2.70	Won			124.5	249
236	1.30	1.04	1.80	Won	-51	-21		
237	1.23	1.04	1.70	Won	-49	-19		
238	1.27	1.04	1.60	Won	-51	-21		
239	1.26	1.04	1.54	Won	-51	-21		
240	1.26	1.04	1.52	Won	-51	-21		
241	1.36	1.04	1.43	Won	-51	-21		
242	1.30	1.04	1.76	Won	-51	-21		
243	1.32	1.04	1000.00	Lost			124.5	
244	1.22	1.04	1.39	Won	-48	-18		
245	1.43	1.03	95.00	Lost			124.5	
246	1.47	1.03	4.10	Won			124.5	249
247	1.27	1.03	4.00	Lost			124.5	
248	1.34	1.03	2.02	Won			124.5	249
249	1.33	1.03	2.00	Lost			124.5	
250	1.41	1.03	2.08	Won			124.5	249
251	1.38	1.03	2.02	Won			124.5	249
252	1.33	1.02	1000.00	Lost			124.5	
253	1.40	1.02	2.78	Won			124.5	249
254	1.22	1.02	1.25	Won	-48	-18		
255	1.26	1.02	1000.00	Lost			124.5	
256	1.45	1.01	1000.00	Lost			124.5	
257	1.39	1.01	1000.00	Lost			124.5	
258	1.36	1.01	12.00	Lost			124.5	
259	1.31	1.01	5.30	Won			124.5	249
260	1.33	1.01	4.10	Won			124.5	249
261	1.34	1.01	1.47	Won	-51	-21		
262	1.38	1.01	10.00	Lost			124.5	
263	1.25	1.01	1000.00	Lost			124.5	
264	1.33	1.01	2.32	Won			124.5	249
265	1.38	1.01	1.57	Won	-51	-21		
266	1.50	1.00	1.00	Won	-51	-51		
267	1.45	1.00	1.00	Won	-51	-51		

268	1.44	1.00	1.00	Won	-51	-51			
269	1.44	1.00	1.00	Won	-51	-51			
270	1.43	1.00	1.00	Won	-51	-51			
271	1.42	1.00	1.00	Won	-51	-51			
272	1.40	1.00	1.00	Won	-51	-51			
273	1.40	1.00	1.00	Won	-51	-51			
274	1.38	1.00	1.00	Won	-51	-51			
275	1.38	1.00	1.00	Won	-51	-51			
276	1.38	1.00	1.00	Won	-51	-51			
277	1.38	1.00	1.00	Won	-51	-51			
278	1.37	1.00	1.00	Won	-51	-51			
279	1.34	1.00	1.00	Won	-51	-51			
280	1.34	1.00	1.00	Won	-51	-51			
281	1.28	1.00	1.00	Won	-51	-51			
282	1.28	1.00	1.00	Won	-51	-51			
283	1.27	1.00	1.00	Lost	-51	-51			
284	1.26	1.00	1.00	Won	-51	-51			
285	1.26	1.00	1.00	Won	-51	-51			
286	1.25	1.00	1.00	Won	-51	-51			
287	1.25	1.00	1.00	Won	-51	-51			
288	1.24	1.00	1.00	Won	-50	-50			
289	1.23	1.00	1.00	Won	-49	-49			
290	1.21	1.00	1.00	Lost	-47	-47			
291	1.50	1.00	1.00	Won	-51	-51			
292	1.31	1.00	1.00	Won	-51	-51			
293	1.20	1.00	1.00	Won	-46	-46			
294	1.43	1.00	1.00	Won	-51	-51			
295	1.49	1.00	1.00	Won	-51	-51			
296	1.36	1.00	1.00	Won	-51	-51			
297	1.26	1.00	1.00	Won	-51	-51			
298	1.32	1.00	1.00	Won	-51	-51			
299	1.48	1.00	1.00	Won	-51	-51			
300	1.43	1.00	1.00	Won	-51	-51			
301	1.24	1.00	1.00	Won	-50	-50			
302	1.49	1.00	1.00	Won	-51	-51			
303	1.42	1.00	1.00	Won	-51	-51			
304	1.37	1.00	1.00	Won	-51	-51			
305	1.20	1.00	1.00	Won	-46	-46			
					Losers	Stop Loss 1.10	Green Up @2	Back @ 2.00	
					-6209	-3999	13059	13309	Winnings
							12406	12644	Commission
							6197	6435	Profit
							13059	13309	Winnings with stop loss
							12406	12644	Commission
							8407	8645	Profit

Back at 1.50 strategy

Here is a description of each column.

- **Column A** is the starting price or available lay price of the favourite prior to going in-play.

- **Column B** is the low price it hit before rising.

- **Column C** is the highest price the selection hit.

- **Column D** highlights whether the favourite won or lost.

- **Column E** shows the losing trades and how much would have been lost on each trade.

- **Column F** shows what happens to the losing trades and how much would have been lost on each trade after employing the stop loss rule.

- **Column G** shows those trades that hit 1.50 and you then went on to green up at 1.50. It also highlights the amount that would have been won on that trade.

- **Column H** shows those trades that hit 1.50 and a straight back bet was then placed. It also highlights the amount that would have been won on that trade.

	A	B	C	D	E	F	G	H
	PRICE	LOW	HIGH	WON /LOST	LOSERS	STOP LOSS 1.10	Green Up @1.50	BACK @ 1.50
1]	1.50	1.50	1.57	Won				
2	1.49	1.46	1000.00	Lost				
3	1.48	1.45	1000.00	Lost				
4	1.48	1.45	1.65	Won				
5	1.45	1.45	1.55	Won				
6	1.50	1.45	5.30	Won				
7	1.46	1.44	1000.00	Lost				
8	1.44	1.44	32.00	Lost				
9	1.50	1.44	1.80	Won				
10	1.50	1.43	1000.00	Won				
11	1.47	1.43	1.55	Won				
12	1.45	1.43	1.47	Won				
13	1.50	1.42	2.02	Won				
14	1.43	1.42	1.57	Won				
15	1.50	1.42	1.61	Won				
16	1.50	1.42	1000.00	Lost				
17	1.41	1.41	1.42	Won				
18	1.43	1.41	1.77	Won				
19	1.49	1.40	1.54	Won				
20	1.45	1.40	1.62	Won				
21	1.40	1.40	1.55	Won				
22	1.44	1.40	1.55	Won				
23	1.44	1.40	1.58	Won				
24	1.42	1.39	1.65	Won				
25	1.46	1.39	1.50	Won				
26	1.44	1.38	1.95	Won				
27	1.42	1.38	1000.00	Lost				
28	1.39	1.38	1.42	Won				
29	1.41	1.38	1.60	Won				
30	1.39	1.38	1.55	Won				
31	1.40	1.37	1.51	Won				
32	1.45	1.37	1.49	Won				
33	1.50	1.36	1000.00	Lost				
34	1.47	1.36	3.50	Won				
35	1.41	1.36	12.00	Lost				
36	1.41	1.36	4.20	Won				
37	1.38	1.36	1.46	Won				
38	1.46	1.36	1.69	Won				
39	1.39	1.36	1.70	Won				
40	1.49	1.36	2.06	Won				
41	1.46	1.36	1000.00	Lost				
42	1.49	1.35	100.00	Lost				
43	1.48	1.35	1.54	Won				
44	1.44	1.35	2.20	Won				
45	1.42	1.35	2.26	Won				
46	1.42	1.35	1.46	Won				
47	1.38	1.35	1000.00	Lost				
48	1.35	1.35	1.37	Won				
49	1.50	1.35	100.00	Lost				

50	1.44	1.35	1000.00	Lost					
51	1.41	1.35	2.22	Won					
52	1.40	1.34	1.52	Won					
53	1.38	1.34	65.00	Lost					
54	1.38	1.34	1000.00	Lost					
55	1.44	1.33	40.00	Lost					
56	1.42	1.33	1.61	Won					
57	1.37	1.33	2.62	Won					
58	1.36	1.33	1.40	Won					
59	1.34	1.33	1.43	Won					
60	1.38	1.33	1.48	Won					
61	1.34	1.32	4.00	Won					
62	1.50	1.32	1000.00	Lost					
63	1.41	1.32	2.08	Won					
64	1.39	1.32	1.87	Won					
65	1.37	1.32	2.00	Won					
66	1.34	1.32	1000.00	Lost					
67	1.34	1.32	1.48	Won					
68	1.40	1.32	1.56	Won					
69	1.36	1.32	1.79	Won					
70	1.50	1.31	5.10	Won					
71	1.37	1.31	1000.00	Lost					
72	1.40	1.31	1000.00	Lost					
73	1.40	1.30	1.69	Won					
74	1.39	1.30	1.74	Won					
75	1.39	1.30	1.72	Won					
76	1.39	1.30	1.60	Won					
77	1.37	1.30	1.50	Won					
78	1.36	1.30	1.74	Won					
79	1.32	1.30	1.50	Won					
80	1.30	1.30	55.00	Lost					
81	1.34	1.30	1000.00	Lost					
82	1.42	1.30	1.43	Won					
83	1.35	1.30	1000.00	Lost					
84	1.37	1.30	1.40	Won					
85	1.50	1.29	1000.00	Lost					
86	1.48	1.29	2.84	Won					
87	1.39	1.29	3.40	Won					
88	1.31	1.29	1.70	Won					
89	1.44	1.29	1000.00	Won					
90	1.36	1.29	1000.00	Lost					
91	1.46	1.28	200.00	Lost					
92	1.31	1.28	5.50	Won					
93	1.31	1.28	1.36	Won					
94	1.48	1.28	1.59	Won					
95	1.39	1.28	1.43	Won					
96	1.38	1.28	6.80	Won					
97	1.42	1.27	25.00	Lost					
98	1.38	1.27	1.72	Won					
99	1.30	1.27	1.34	Won					
100	1.35	1.27	1.42	Won					
101	1.31	1.27	1.55	Won					
102	1.34	1.27	6.60	Won					
103	1.35	1.27	2.80	Won					
104	1.32	1.27	1.80	Won					
105	1.38	1.26	1.56	Won					

					Losers	Stop Loss 1.10	Green Up @1.5	Back @ 1.5
106	1.27	1.26	1.30	Won				
107	1.47	1.26	3.70	Won				
108	1.45	1.26	20.00	Won				
109	1.43	1.26	1.74	Won				
110	1.37	1.26	1.43	Won				
111	1.33	1.26	1.92	Won	Losers	Stop Loss 1.10	Green Up @1.5	Back @ 1.5

1	1.38	1.25	400.00	Lost			16.66	
2	1.46	1.25	2.68	Won			16.66	25
3	1.30	1.25	1.76	Won			16.66	25
4	1.41	1.25	1.69	Won			16.66	25
5	1.30	1.25	1.34	Won	-25	-15		
6	1.26	1.25	1.27	Won	-25	-15		
7	1.38	1.25	500.00	Lost			16.66	
8	1.30	1.25	55.00	Lost			16.66	
9	1.46	1.25	4.60	Won			16.66	25
10	1.50	1.25	1.59	Won			16.66	25
11	1.35	1.25	1.82	Won			16.66	25
12	1.30	1.25	150.00	Lost			16.66	
13	1.29	1.25	3.70	Won			16.66	25
14	1.29	1.25	1.36	Won	-25	-15		
15	1.26	1.24	5.00	Won			16.66	25
16	1.39	1.24	1.70	Won			16.66	25
17	1.43	1.24	1.50	Won			16.66	25
18	1.27	1.24	1.38	Won	-25	-15		
19	1.26	1.24	1.35	Won	-25	-15		
20	1.24	1.24	1.32	Won	-24	-14		
21	1.33	1.24	1000.00	Lost			16.66	
22	1.46	1.23	3.15	Won			16.66	25
23	1.40	1.23	2.12	Won			16.66	25
24	1.33	1.23	1.62	Won			16.66	25
25	1.33	1.23	1.50	Won			16.66	25
26	1.29	1.23	1.43	Won	-25	-15		
27	1.29	1.23	1.34	Won	-25	-15		
28	1.24	1.23	1.28	Won	-24	-14		
29	1.39	1.23	6.00	Lost			16.66	
30	1.29	1.22	1000.00	Lost			16.66	
31	1.23	1.22	8.00	Won			16.66	25
32	1.38	1.22	2.44	Won			16.66	25
33	1.39	1.22	1.80	Won			16.66	25
34	1.28	1.22	1.31	Won	-25	-15		
35	1.24	1.22	1.30	Won	-24	-14		
36	1.32	1.22	1000.00	Lost			16.66	
37	1.49	1.21	1000.00	Won			16.66	25
38	1.48	1.21	1000.00	Won			16.66	25
39	1.36	1.21	1000.00	Lost			16.66	
40	1.29	1.21	90.00	Lost			16.66	
41	1.29	1.21	2.32	Won			16.66	25
42	1.31	1.21	1.77	Won			16.66	25

43	1.45	1.21	1.62	Won			16.66	25
44	1.22	1.21	1.58	Won			16.66	25
45	1.30	1.21	1.45	Won	−25	−15		
46	1.31	1.21	1.40	Won	−25	−15		
47	1.29	1.21	1.35	Won	−25	−15		
48	1.23	1.21	1.32	Won	−23	−13		
49	1.24	1.21	1.30	Won	−24	−14		
50	1.25	1.21	3.30	Won			16.66	25
51	1.33	1.21	110.00	Lost			16.66	
52	1.36	1.21	1000.00	Lost			16.66	
53	1.29	1.21	1.38	Won	−25	−15		
54	1.42	1.21	1.58	Won			16.66	25
55	1.23	1.21	1.35	Won	−23	−13		
56	1.23	1.20	150.00	Won			18	27
57	1.42	1.20	80.00	Lost			16.66	
58	1.49	1.20	4.30	Won			16.66	25
59	1.36	1.20	3.00	Won			16.66	25
60	1.39	1.20	2.68	Won			16.66	25
61	1.36	1.20	2.02	Won			16.66	25
62	1.22	1.20	2.00	Won			18.66	28
63	1.24	1.20	1.95	Won			17.33	26
64	1.22	1.20	1.89	Won			18.66	28
65	1.29	1.20	1.46	Won	−25	−15		
66	1.24	1.20	1.43	Won	−24	−14		
67	1.38	1.20	1000.00	Lost			16.66	
68	1.28	1.20	1.59	Won			16.66	25
69	1.21	1.20	1.68	Won			19.33	29
70	1.45	1.20	2.22	Won			16.66	25
71	1.45	1.20	1000.00	Lost			16.66	
72	1.38	1.20	1000.00	Lost			16.66	
73	1.30	1.20	1.42	Won	−25	−15		
74	1.23	1.20	1.24	Won	−23	−13		
75	1.23	1.19	1000.00	Lost			16.66	
76	1.23	1.19	250.00	Lost			16.66	
77	1.22	1.19	1.76	Won			18.66	28
78	1.21	1.19	1.50	Won			19.33	29
79	1.29	1.19	1.35	Won	−25	−15		
80	1.20	1.19	1.23	Won	−20	−10		
81	1.24	1.19	1.30	Won	−24	−14		
82	1.27	1.19	1.35	Won	−25	−15		
83	1.20	1.19	1.21	Won	−20	−10		
84	1.50	1.18	1000.00	Lost			16.66	
85	1.31	1.18	1000.00	Lost			16.66	
86	1.24	1.18	120.00	Lost			16.66	
87	1.30	1.18	1.59	Won			16.66	25
88	1.29	1.18	1.45	Won	−25	−15		
89	1.21	1.18	1.22	Won	−21	−11		
90	1.20	1.18	1.24	Won	−20	−10		
91	1.31	1.17	26.00	Won			16.66	25
92	1.21	1.17	2.36	Won			19.33	29
93	1.38	1.17	2.20	Won			16.66	25
94	1.36	1.17	1.70	Won			16.66	25
95	1.29	1.17	1.67	Won			16.66	25
96	1.23	1.17	1.25	Won	−23	−13		
97	1.32	1.17	3.50	Won			16.66	25
98	1.27	1.17	2.20	Won			16.66	25

99	1.21	1.17	1.31	Won	-21	-11		
100	1.29	1.16	1000.00	Lost			16.66	
101	1.21	1.16	2.22	Won			19.33	29
102	1.22	1.16	1.66	Won			18.66	28
103	1.34	1.16	1.40	Won	-25	-15		
104	1.25	1.16	1.31	Won	-25	-15		
105	1.38	1.16	5.00	Won			16.66	25
106	1.31	1.16	2.08	Won			16.66	25
107	1.42	1.15	80.00	Lost			16.66	
108	1.21	1.15	50.00	Lost			16.66	
109	1.42	1.15	14.00	Lost			16.66	
110	1.38	1.15	4.30	Lost			16.66	
111	1.34	1.15	3.50	Won			16.66	25
112	1.21	1.15	3.25	Won			14.5	29
113	1.30	1.15	1.50	Won			16.66	25
114	1.21	1.15	1.45	Won	-21	-11		
115	1.38	1.15	1.44	Won	-25	-15		
116	1.25	1.15	1.29	Won	-25	-15		
117	1.27	1.15	1.31	Won	-25	-15		
118	1.38	1.15	2.00	Won			16.66	25
119	1.37	1.15	4.00	Won			16.66	25
120	1.20	1.15	1.62	Won			20	30
121	1.40	1.14	1000.00	Lost			16.66	
122	1.48	1.14	2.82	Won			16.66	25
123	1.39	1.14	1.79	Won			16.66	25
124	1.49	1.14	1.76	Won			16.66	25
125	1.34	1.14	2.62	Won			16.66	25
126	1.24	1.14	300.00	Lost			16.66	
127	1.20	1.14	1.68	Won			20	30
128	1.39	1.13	200.00	Lost			66	
129	1.46	1.13	9.20	Lost			66	
130	1.48	1.13	2.78	Won			66	99
131	1.36	1.13	2.10	Won			66	99
132	1.33	1.13	1.75	Won			66	99
133	1.39	1.13	1.55	Won			66	99
134	1.21	1.13	1.29	Won	-47	-17		
135	1.50	1.13	120.00	Lost			66	
136	1.32	1.13	2.02	Won			66	99
137	1.40	1.12	1000.00	Lost			66	
138	1.40	1.12	1000.00	Lost			66	
139	1.30	1.12	55.00	Lost			66	
140	1.35	1.12	4.10	Won			66	99
141	1.39	1.12	2.50	Won			66	99
142	1.49	1.12	2.26	Won			66	99
143	1.23	1.12	2.12	Won			67.33	101
144	1.49	1.12	2.00	Won			66	99
145	1.46	1.12	1.65	Won			66	99
146	1.44	1.12	1.52	Won			66	99
147	1.33	1.12	1.46	Won	-51	-21		
148	1.23	1.12	1.26	Won	-49	-19		
149	1.44	1.12	2.44	Won			66	99
150	1.33	1.12	1.60	Won			66	99
151	1.26	1.12	1.66	Won			66	99
152	1.31	1.12	160.00	Lost	-51	-21		
153	1.40	1.12	1000.00	Lost			66	
154	1.20	1.12	1.23	Won	-46	-16		

155	1.31	1.11	1000.00	Lost			66	
156	1.22	1.11	1000.00	Lost			66	
157	1.22	1.11	100.00	Lost			66	
158	1.45	1.11	5.10	Won			66	99
159	1.26	1.11	2.50	Won			66	99
160	1.36	1.11	2.20	Won			66	99
161	1.45	1.11	2.00	Won			66	99
162	1.48	1.11	1.55	Won			66	99
163	1.25	1.11	1.43	Won	−51	−21		
164	1.33	1.11	70.00	Lost			66	
165	1.30	1.11	1.51	Won			66	99
166	1.36	1.11	90.00	Lost			66	
167	1.49	1.11	4.60	Won			66	99
168	1.27	1.11	1.73	Won			66	99
169	1.21	1.11	1.53	Won			68.66	103
170	1.48	1.10	15.00	Lost			66	
171	1.35	1.10	2.10	Won			66	99
172	1.49	1.10	2.00	Won			66	99
173	1.27	1.10	1.87	Won	−51	−21		
174	1.35	1.10	2.00	Won			66	99
175	1.30	1.10	1.37	Won	−51	−21		
176	1.45	1.10	1000.00	Lost			66	
177	1.30	1.10	1.65	Won			66	99
178	1.24	1.10	1000.00	Lost			66	
179	1.41	1.09	1000.00	Lost			66	
180	1.41	1.09	1000.00	Lost			66	
181	1.34	1.09	32.00	Lost			66	
182	1.29	1.09	10.00	Won			66	99
183	1.34	1.09	5.00	Lost			66	
184	1.36	1.09	3.80	Won			66	99
185	1.20	1.09	2.36	Won			69.33	104
186	1.37	1.09	2.00	Won			66	99
187	1.36	1.09	1.81	Won			66	99
188	1.36	1.09	1.76	Won			66	99
189	1.23	1.09	1.60	Won			67.33	101
190	1.25	1.09	1.30	Won	−51	−21		
191	1.23	1.09	1.26	Won	−51	−21		
192	1.34	1.09	21.00	Lost			66	
193	1.27	1.09	1.40	Won	−51	−21		
194	1.28	1.08	11.00	Lost			66	
195	1.33	1.08	1.75	Won			66	99
196	1.24	1.08	1.44	Won	−50	−20		
197	1.33	1.08	1.35	Won	−51	−21		
198	1.29	1.08	1.50	Won			66	99
199	1.21	1.08	6.00	Won			66	99
200	1.40	1.08	1.81	Won			66	99
201	1.23	1.08	1.45	Won	−49	−19		
202	1.37	1.07	1000.00	Won			66	99
203	1.21	1.07	1000.00	Lost			66	
204	1.38	1.07	100.00	Lost			66	
205	1.43	1.07	5.00	Lost			66	
206	1.44	1.07	2.42	Won			66	99
207	1.22	1.07	1.41	Won	−48	−18		
208	1.23	1.07	1.35	Won	−49	−19		
209	1.21	1.07	1.30	Won	−46	−16		
210	1.34	1.07	1.44	Won	−51	−21		

211	1.27	1.07	1.30	Won	−51	−21		
212	1.28	1.06	1000.00	Lost			66	
213	1.39	1.06	2.08	Won			66	99
214	1.34	1.06	1.64	Won			66	99
215	1.21	1.06	1.60	Won			68.66	103
216	1.39	1.06	2.20	Won			66	99
217	1.28	1.06	4.80	Won			66	99
218	1.50	1.05	1000.00	Lost			66	
219	1.32	1.05	1000.00	Lost			66	
220	1.34	1.05	5.00	Lost			66	
221	1.36	1.05	3.65	Won			66	99
222	1.23	1.05	2.12	Won			67.33	101
223	1.35	1.05	2.08	Won			66	99
224	1.37	1.05	1.72	Won			66	99
225	1.42	1.05	1.63	Won			66	99
226	1.35	1.05	2.28	Won			66	99
227	1.28	1.05	2.80	Won			66	99
228	1.46	1.05	990.00	Lost			66	
229	1.31	1.05	2.20	Won			66	99
230	1.25	1.05	50.00	Lost			66	
231	1.25	1.05	2.72	Won			66	99
232	1.32	1.04	1000.00	Lost			66	
233	1.33	1.04	5.00	Lost			66	
234	1.27	1.04	5.00	Won			66	99
235	1.45	1.04	2.70	Won			66	99
236	1.30	1.04	1.80	Won			66	99
237	1.23	1.04	1.70	Won			67.33	101
238	1.27	1.04	1.60	Won			66	99
239	1.26	1.04	1.54	Won			66	99
240	1.26	1.04	1.52	Won			66	99
241	1.36	1.04	1.43	Won	−51	−21		
242	1.30	1.04	1.76	Won			66	99
243	1.32	1.04	1000.00	Lost			66	
244	1.22	1.04	1.39	Won	−48	−18		
245	1.43	1.03	95.00	Lost			66	
246	1.47	1.03	4.10	Won			66	99
247	1.27	1.03	4.00	Lost			66	
248	1.34	1.03	2.02	Won			66	99
249	1.33	1.03	2.00	Lost			66	
250	1.41	1.03	2.08	Won			66	99
251	1.38	1.03	2.02	Won			66	99
252	1.33	1.02	1000.00	Lost			66	
253	1.40	1.02	2.78	Won			66	99
254	1.22	1.02	1.25	Won	−48	−18		
255	1.26	1.02	1000.00	Lost			66	
256	1.45	1.01	1000.00	Lost			66	
257	1.39	1.01	1000.00	Lost			66	
258	1.36	1.01	12.00	Lost			66	
259	1.31	1.01	5.30	Won			66	99
260	1.33	1.01	4.10	Won			66	99
261	1.34	1.01	1.47	Won	−51	−21		
262	1.38	1.01	10.00	Lost			66	
263	1.25	1.01	1000.00	Lost			66	
264	1.33	1.01	2.32	Won			66	99
265	1.38	1.01	1.57	Won			66	99
266	1.50	1.00	1.00	Won	−51	−51		

267	1.45	1.00	1.00	Won	-51	-51			
268	1.44	1.00	1.00	Won	-51	-51			
269	1.44	1.00	1.00	Won	-51	-51			
270	1.43	1.00	1.00	Won	-51	-51			
271	1.42	1.00	1.00	Won	-51	-51			
272	1.40	1.00	1.00	Won	-51	-51			
273	1.40	1.00	1.00	Won	-51	-51			
274	1.38	1.00	1.00	Won	-51	-51			
275	1.38	1.00	1.00	Won	-51	-51			
276	1.38	1.00	1.00	Won	-51	-51			
277	1.38	1.00	1.00	Won	-51	-51			
278	1.37	1.00	1.00	Won	-51	-51			
279	1.34	1.00	1.00	Won	-51	-51			
280	1.34	1.00	1.00	Won	-51	-51			
281	1.28	1.00	1.00	Won	-51	-51			
282	1.28	1.00	1.00	Won	-51	-51			
283	1.27	1.00	1.00	Lost	-51	-51			
284	1.26	1.00	1.00	Won	-51	-51			
285	1.26	1.00	1.00	Won	-51	-51			
286	1.25	1.00	1.00	Won	-51	-51			
287	1.25	1.00	1.00	Won	-51	-51			
288	1.24	1.00	1.00	Won	-50	-50			
289	1.23	1.00	1.00	Won	-49	-49			
290	1.21	1.00	1.00	Lost	-47	-47			
291	1.50	1.00	1.00	Won	-51	-51			
292	1.31	1.00	1.00	Won	-51	-51			
293	1.20	1.00	1.00	Won	-46	-46			
294	1.43	1.00	1.00	Won	-51	-51			
295	1.49	1.00	1.00	Won	-51	-51			
296	1.36	1.00	1.00	Won	-51	-51			
297	1.26	1.00	1.00	Won	-51	-51			
298	1.32	1.00	1.00	Won	-51	-51			
299	1.48	1.00	1.00	Won	-51	-51			
300	1.43	1.00	1.00	Won	-51	-51			
301	1.24	1.00	1.00	Won	-50	-50			
302	1.49	1.00	1.00	Won	-51	-51			
303	1.42	1.00	1.00	Won	-51	-51			
304	1.37	1.00	1.00	Won	-51	-51			
305	1.20	1.00	1.00	Won	-46	-46			
					Losers	Stop Loss 1.10	Green Up @1.5	Back @ 1.5	
					-4074	-3004	9112	8719	Winnings
							8656	8283	Commission
							4582	4209	PROFIT
							9112	8719	Winnings with Stop Loss
							8656	8283	Commission
							5652	5279	Profit

III. Explanation of Charts Used in the Book

Throughout the book you will see charts that represent the in-play price movement of the market highlighted. These charts are my personal interpretation of the price movement and are compiled from various sources. The charts are designed to give the reader a general indication of the price movement during that event.

They do not highlight every price that may have been traded in the event.

I can, however, state that the price relating to the key points in relation to the text and rules advised in the strategies were actually traded.

Betfair historical data

If you require a more detailed analysis, and a definitive guide on all of the prices traded during an event, then historical data can be accessed at data.betfair.com.

Betfair also have a third party vendor called Fracsoft (www.fracsoft.com). Their data is an exact replica of what Betfair users see using the website to view the Betfair market.

You can purchase the data by market – for example, a typical horse racing market costs around 60p to purchase. I would certainly suggest if you are analysing in-play horse racing markets that this is the best option as, due to the speed of the price movement in these markets, it is impossible to record with complete accuracy in any other way.

Charts available on the Betfair site

As a (free) alternative, and to give you an indication of how a player/team has moved within a market and how a market behaves during an event, you could do the following.

In the example below we are looking at the Andy Murray v Fernando González market.

Once in the Betfair site, go to the market you require and click on the icon just to the left of the player or team name.

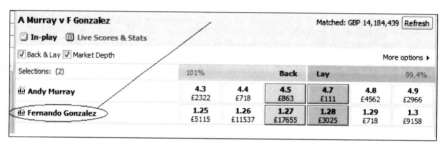

You will then be presented with a screen like the one shown below.

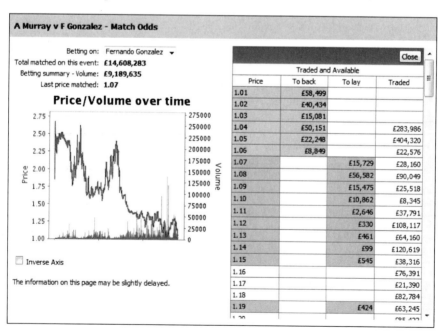

This screen shows a chart of the price movement of Fernando González. It also highlights the amount of money traded and the money available to back and lay.

This information can be used to good effect, as you can then see the general movement of the price and also confirm the price traded on your selection.

Also, if you wait for the match to end you can save a screenshot of the chart (which you can refer to later).

Chart headings & reference points

I want to point out a couple of things with reference to the chart headings and reference points that are presented in this book.

The charts represent the following –

- The charts record the in-play price available during the event
- The y axis is the price/odds available for the highlighted selection
- The x axis represents each 10 second point

The chart title refers to the competitors and the final score of the contest.

In the example below we have the match between Aleksandra Wozniak and Julia Goerges.

Aleksandra Wozniak v Julia Goerges (6-7, 6-3) WTA Warsaw Open Monday 18th May 2009

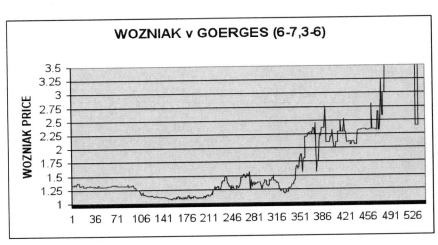

You will see on the title it states Wozniak v Goerges (6-7, 6-3). This means that Wozniak lost 6 games to 7 in the 1st set and 3 games to 6 in the 2nd set. Therefore she lost the match 2-0.

It should also be noted that the charts mainly highlight the favourite of that event. The reason for this is that under normal circumstances that is where the majority of the money is generally traded and that is what most of the strategies presented in this book are based upon (i.e. laying low-priced favourites).

IV. Odds Comparison Chart

The table below shows the corresponding odds to equal 100% to be used when trying to obtain better odds on Betfair.

For example, if a back selection is priced up at 1.81: if you then lay at 2.22 you are effectively backing at 1.82.

Back Price	Lay Price	Back Price	Lay Price
1.60	2.67	1.96	2.04
1.61	2.64	1.97	2.03
1.62	2.61	1.98	2.02
1.63	2.59	1.99	2.01
1.64	2.56	2.00	2.00
1.65	2.54	2.02	1.98
1.66	2.52	2.04	1.96
1.67	2.49	2.06	1.94
1.68	2.47	2.08	1.93
1.69	2.45	2.10	1.91
1.70	2.43	2.12	1.89
1.71	2.41	2.14	1.88
1.72	2.39	2.16	1.86
1.73	2.37	2.18	1.85
1.74	2.35	2.20	1.83
1.75	2.33	2.22	1.82
1.76	2.32	2.24	1.81
1.77	2.30	2.26	1.79
1.78	2.28	2.28	1.78
1.79	2.27	2.30	1.77
1.80	2.25	2.32	1.76
1.81	2.23	2.34	1.75
1.82	2.22	2.36	1.74
1.83	2.20	2.38	1.72
1.84	2.19	2.40	1.71
1.85	2.18	2.42	1.70
1.86	2.16	2.44	1.69
1.87	2.15	2.46	1.68
1.88	2.14	2.48	1.68
1.89	2.12	2.50	1.67
1.90	2.11	2.52	1.66
1.91	2.10	2.54	1.65
1.92	2.09	2.56	1.64
1.93	2.08	2.58	1.63
1.94	2.06	2.60	1.63
1.95	2.05	2.62	1.62

V. Resources

I list below resources that I use myself and would recommend to others – you can never have enough information!

Betting exchanges

Betfair (www.betfair.com)

The number one betting exchange in the world. Currently without any serious rivals to its position.

Betdaq (www.betdaq.com)

There is nothing wrong with Betdaq; indeed, I recommend opening an account with them, as sometimes you can receive better odds. Obviously liquidity can be an issue; but if you can get your initial trade on at a better price, then you will certainly be able to lay off on Betfair.

Also, with the introduction of Betfair's premium charge, there has been a noticeable increase in the amount of money available to trade on Betdaq.

Betting blogs and forums

There are quite a few blogs that are dedicated to the betting exchanges, all of which provide interesting reading. The main problem with these blogs is that they can come and go depending on whether the author can be bothered to update them. Because of this I am not going to mention specific blogs here, but instead I suggest that you go to petenordsted.com where you will find a list of all current and recommended trading and sports-related blogs.

I would also recommend reading the Betfair forums. Many of the forums highlight some good ideas.

Software

Bet Angel (www.betangel.com)

Go to their website and check out the features of this excellent software.

Bettorlogic (www.bettorlogic.com)

I really like this site and it is certainly my first stop when it comes to analysing the football markets – where their weekly stats football tables and match sections are second to none. The site covers football, golf, rugby union, formula one and tennis. Although I believe the site is best used for those who are having a straight bet, it is very useful for analysing a market before going in-play.

Their Form Lab feature is excellent, and I always use this to compile my own odds before the weekend's football.

Media

Racing Post (www.racingpost.com)

I always refer to the website and purchase the publication at weekends as it is very useful for identifying pre-match sentiment. For example, if the *Racing Post*, believes that a match will end over 2.5 goals, I will never consider backing under 2.5 goals no matter what the stats are telling me. Obviously it is different if you are trading in-play, but if you are trading only pre-match you have to take notice of the recommendations because of the number of readers this publication attracts.

Sport-specific websites

Football

There are plenty of sites dedicated to football stats of which a number are highlighted below. All are fairly similar; however, once again, I do prefer Bettorlogic.

- www.bettorlogic.com

- www.soccerway.com

- www.soccerstats.com

- www.football365.com

- www.soccerbase.com

- www.football-data.co.uk

- www.statto.com

Another resource I like to look at is the Fink Tank predictor which can be found at the following link:

- www.timesonline.co.uk/tol/sport/football/fink_tank/

The articles are always well written and the predictor is also interesting to use.

Golf

As previously discussed earlier in the book, following golf live, especially on the United States circuit, can be extremely frustrating, as the 'live' pictures provided by Eurosport and Sky rarely are. Although I do watch the TV coverage, I tend to follow the US PGA events on the website, as sometimes information appears there before it does on the TV. The tour websites are also a great resource for telling you which are the hardest holes on the course, and how each player has played them in the past rounds.

I also like the subscription site tour-tips, with its extensive database. The great thing about the database is that you can see exactly how a player has performed whilst, for example, being within four shots of the lead with a round to go. This is useful because it highlights those players who tend to 'choke' in the final round. It also highlights course specialists. This is a good resource alongside the golfing previews provided by Bettorlogic and the *Racing Post*.

- www.pgatour.com

- www.europeantour.com

- www.tour-tips.com

Cricket

Cricinfo provides scorecards and statistics on all versions of the game that go back through the history of the game. The site is extremely useful when planning which matches and events you are going to trade, as it holds a comprehensive fixture list.

They feature live scorecards, but in truth I would only trade using these scorecards for test matches. The one-day matches move far too fast to make trading using just the updated scorecard a viable option, and I would certainly only rely on TV pictures to update you on events.

- www.cricinfo.com

Tennis

- www.atpworldtour.com

- www.sonyericssonwtatour.com

- tennis-data.co.uk

I find these sites invaluable, especially when I am trading looking for a tournament winner. These sites detail the all-important order of play, as well as providing links to live scoreboards and stats such as percentage of service games won and break points converted, etc.

Another useful tool is the Mort Hill in-play tennis calculator, which highlights what the odds should be given the starting price and current score in the match. I personally don't use the calculator during a match, but it is an extremely useful tool in highlighting the massive change in odds that can be gained in just a few points.

- mort-hill-in-play-tennis-calculator.smartcode.com/info.html

Books

There are many fine books dedicated to trading the financial markets, but very few dedicated to the sporting markets. As you will now have seen, trading is trading, and the books I have highlighted below show how you can implement the rules used in the financial markets for the sporting markets:

Trading in the Zone, by Mark Douglas

The Disciplined Trader, by Mark Douglas

The books highlight the fact that, once you place your money in the market, anything can and will happen. These two books completely changed the way I approach both my sporting and financial trading, and I cannot recommend them highly enough.

I also enjoyed this account of Iain Fletcher's year on the betting exchanges, and would certainly recommend it as a holiday read:

Game, Set and Matched, by Iain Fletcher

Advice, strategies and systems

Pete Nordsted (www.petenordsted.com)

I have a real passion for trading and post my latest thoughts on my personal blog.

I am also available to point you in the right direction should you require any further trading advice. For an initial consultation regarding any aspect of trading on Betfair please email me via:

- masteringbetfair@petenordsted.com
- www.petenordsted.com
- twitter.com/petenordsted

Premier Betting (www.premier-betting.com)

Premier Betting is the brand new website for football punters from top sports bettors Pete Nordsted and Matt Finnigan.

Premier Betting gives the edge back to the punter by highlighting through our ratings the best value bets in all the popular markets for upcoming Premiership games.

When combining our unique ratings with our exclusive expert analysis you can be assured that you are placing your money on the best value selections every weekend.

Entry level for the ratings and analysis is only £7 per month.

The X Report (www.petenordsted.com)

Give yourself real edge over other traders in the Betfair markets by subscribing to the X Report (£15 per month).

The X Report is a monthly report compiled by myself.

Over the past few years I have spent a great deal of time studying the price movements in the Betfair markets, and it is through this analysis that I have devised numerous profitable trading strategies.

This information will be unavailable anywhere else.

If you do not have time to either devise or back test any strategies then this is the document for you as I do all of the work for you.

By subscribing to the X Report you will receive a document that contains both statistics and full analysis of major upcoming sporting events.

The exclusive information contained in this report will give you a real advantage over other traders in the market. And it will ensure that you are in a position to fully profit from my findings.

Trading blindly without a plan can be very costly.

Sign up to the X Report and trade with the professionals.

The X Club (xclub.proxtrading.com)

The X Club is the brainchild of Matt Finnigan, a full-time professional trader on the Betfair markets.

Matt could not only see that there was a void in the market for quality education. He also found that trading full time could be a very solitary existence and so he decided to start a trading club and share the strategies he uses with the members.

Today traders who buy into the concept of the X Club are joining the most exclusive club on the web.

And the concept is simple.

1. Join the X Club and read the manual.

2. Trade the strategies contained in the manual.

3. Be mentored by a full-time trader until you are comfortable trading the strategies.

4. Become a successful trader and share your knowledge and ideas with other members.

If you are interested in joining the X Club email me at masteringbetfair@petenordsted.com for a preferential rate.

Once the club reaches 100 members then the doors will close and anyone wishing to join will be put on a waiting list.

Index